Abraham Lincoln

Message of the President of the United States and Reports

Proper of the Heads of Departments

Made at the Second Session of the Thirty-Seventh Congress

Abraham Lincoln

Message of the President of the United States and Reports Proper of the Heads of Departments
Made at the Second Session of the Thirty-Seventh Congress

ISBN/EAN: 9783337877408

Printed in Europe, USA, Canada, Australia, Japan

Cover: Foto ©ninafisch / pixelio.de

More available books at **www.hansebooks.com**

MESSAGE

OF THE

PRESIDENT OF THE UNITED STATES

AND

REPORTS PROPER

OF THE

HEADS OF DEPARTMENTS,

MADE AT

THE SECOND SESSION

OF THE

THIRTY-SEVENTH CONGRESS.

WASHINGTON:
GOVERNMENT PRINTING OFFICE.
1861.

MESSAGE.

Fellow-citizens of the Senate and House of Representatives:

In the midst of unprecedented political troubles, we have cause of great gratitude to God for unusual good health, and most abundant harvests.

You will not be surprised to learn that, in the peculiar exigencies of the times, our intercourse with foreign nations has been attended with profound solicitude, chiefly turning upon our own domestic affairs.

A disloyal portion of the American people have, during the whole year, been engaged in an attempt to divide and destroy the Union. A nation which endures factious domestic division, is exposed to disrespect abroad; and one party, if not both, is sure, sooner or later, to invoke foreign intervention.

Nations thus tempted to interfere, are not always able to resist the counsels of seeming expediency and ungenerous ambition, although measures adopted under such influences seldom fail to be unfortunate and injurious to those adopting them.

The disloyal citizens of the United States who have offered the ruin of our country, in return for the aid and comfort which they have invoked abroad, have received less patronage and encouragement than they probably expected. If it were just to suppose, as the insurgents have seemed to assume, that foreign nations, in this case, discarding all moral, social, and treaty obligations, would act solely, and selfishly, for the most speedy restoration of commerce, including, especially, the acquisition of cotton, those nations appear, as yet, not to. have seen their way to their object more directly, or clearly, through the destruction, than through the preservation, of the Union. If we could dare to believe that foreign nations are actuated by no higher principle than this, I am quite sure a sound argument could be made to show them that they can reach their aim more readily, and easily, by aiding to crush this rebellion, than by giving encouragement to it.

The principal lever relied on by the insurgents for exciting foreign nations to hostility against us, as already intimated, is the embarrassment of commerce. Those nations, however, not improbably, saw from the first, that it was the Union which made, as well our foreign, as our domestic commerce. They can scarcely have failed to perceive that the effort for disunion produces the existing difficulty; and that one strong nation promises more durable peace, and a more extensive, valuable and reliable commerce, than can the same nation broken into hostile fragments.

It is not my purpose to review our discussions with foreign states; because whatever might be their wishes, or dispositions, the integrity of our country, and the stability of our government, mainly depend, not upon them, but on the loyalty, virtue, patriotism, and intelligence of the American people. The correspondence itself, with the usual reservations, is herewith submitted.

I venture to hope it will appear that we have practiced prudence, and liberality towards foreign powers, averting causes of irritation; and, with firmness, maintaining our own rights and honor.

Since, however, it is apparent that here, as in every other state, foreign dangers necessarily attend domestic difficulties, I recommend that adequate and ample measures be adopted for maintaining the public defences on every side. While, under this general recommendation, provision for defending our sea-coast line readily occurs to the mind, I also, in the same connexion, ask the attention of Congress to our great lakes and rivers. It is believed that some fortifications and depots of arms and munitions, with harbor and navigation improvements, all at well selected points upon these, would be of great importance to the national defence and preservation. I ask attention to the views of the Secretary of War, expressed in his report, upon the same general subject.

I deem it of importance that the loyal regions of East Tennessee and western North Carolina should be connected with Kentucky, and other faithful parts of the Union, by railroad. I therefore recommend, as a military measure, that Congress provide for the construction of such road, as speedily as possible. Kentucky, no doubt, will co-operate, and, through her legislature, make the most judicious selection of a line. The northern terminus must connect with some existing railroad; and whether the route shall be from Lexington, or Nicholasville, to the Cumberland Gap; or from Lebanon to the Tennessee line, in the direction of Knoxville; or on some still different line, can easily be determined. Kentucky and the general government co-operating, the work can be completed in a very short time; and when done, it will be not only of vast present usefulness, but also a valuable permanent improvement, worth its cost in all the future.

Some treaties, designed chiefly for the interests of commerce, and having no grave political importance, have been negotiated, and will be submitted to the Senate for their consideration.

Although we have failed to induce some of the commercial powers to adopt a desirable melioration of the rigor of maritime war, we have removed all obstructions from the way of this humane reform, except such as are merely of temporary and accidental occurrence.

I invite your attention to the correspondence between her Britannic Majesty's minister accredited to this government, and the Secretary of State, relative to the detention of the British ship Perthshire in June last, by the United States steamer Massachusetts, for a supposed breach of the blockade. As this detention was occasioned by an obvious misapprehension of the facts, and as justice requires that we should commit no belligerent act not founded in strict right, as sanctioned by public law, I recommend that an appropriation be made to satisfy the reasonable demand of the owners of the vessel for her detention.

I repeat the recommendation of my predecessor, in his annual message to Congress in December last, in regard to the disposition of the surplus which will probably remain after satisfying the claims of American citizens against China, pursuant to the awards of the commissioners under the act of the 3d of March, 1859. If, however, it should not be deemed advisable to carry that recommendation into effect, I would suggest that authority be given for investing the principal, over the proceeds of the surplus referred to, in good securities, with a view to the satisfaction of such other just claims of our citizens against China as are not unlikely to arise hereafter in the course of our extensive trade with that Empire.

By the act of the 5th of August last, Congress authorized the President to instruct the commanders of suitable vessels to defend themselves against, and to capture pirates. This authority has been exercised in a single instance only. For the more effectual protection of our extensive and valuable commerce, in the eastern seas especially, it seems to me that it would also be advisable to authorize the commanders of sailing vessels to re-capture any prizes which pirates may make of United States vessels and their cargoes, and the consular courts, now established by law in eastern countries, to adjudicate the cases, in the event that this should not be objected to by the local authorities.

If any good reason exists why we should persevere longer in withholding our recognition of the independence and sovereignty of Hayti and Liberia, I am unable to discern it. Unwilling, however, to inaugurate a novel policy in regard to them without the approbation of Congress, I submit for your consideration the expediency of an appropriation for maintaining a chargé d'affaires near each of those new states. It does not admit of doubt that important commercial advantages might be secured by favorable treaties with them.

The operations of the treasury during the period which has elapsed since your adjournment have been conducted with signal success. The patriotism of the people has placed at the disposal of the government the large means demanded by the public exigencies. Much of the national loan has been taken by citizens of the industrial classes, whose confidence in their country's faith, and zeal for their country's deliverance from present peril, have induced them to contribute to the support of the government the whole of their limited acquisitions. This fact imposes peculiar obligations to economy in disbursement and energy in action.

The revenue from all sources, including loans, for the financial year ending on the 30th June, 1861, was eighty-six million eight hundred and thirty-five thousand nine hundred dollars and twenty-seven cents, and the expenditures for the same period, including payments on account of the public debt, were eighty-four million five hundred and seventy-eight thousand eight hundred and thirty-four dollars and forty-seven cents; leaving a balance in the treasury, on the 1st July, of two million two hundred and fifty-seven thousand sixty-five dollars and eighty cents. For the first quarter of the financial year, ending on the 30th September, 1861, the receipts from all sources, including the balance of 1st of July, were one hundred and two million five hundred and thirty-two thousand five hundred and nine dollars and twenty-seven cents, and the expenses ninety-eight million two hundred and thirty-nine thousand seven hundred and thirty-three dollars and nine cents; leaving a balance, on the 1st of October, 1861, of four million two hundred and ninety-two thousand seven hundred and seventy-six dollars and eighteen cents.

Estimates for the remaining three quarters of the year, and for the financial year 1863, together with his views of ways and means for meeting the demands contemplated by them, will be submitted to Congress by the Secretary of the Treasury. It is gratifying to know that the expenditures made necessary by the rebellion are not beyond the resources of the loyal people, and to believe that the same patriotism which has thus far sustained the government will continue to sustain it till Peace and Union shall again bless the land.

I respectfully refer to the report of the Secretary of War for information respecting the numerical strength of the army, and for recommendations having in view an increase of its efficiency and the well being of the various branches of the service intrusted to his care. It is gratifying to know that the patriotism of the people has proved equal to the occasion, and that the number of troops tendered greatly exceeds the force which Congress authorized me to call into the field.

I refer with pleasure to those portions of his report which make allusion to the creditable degree of discipline already attained by our troops, and to the excellent sanitary condition of the entire army.

The recommendation of the Secretary for an organization of the militia upon a uniform basis, is a subject of vital importance to the future safety of the country, and is commended to the serious attention of Congress.

The large addition to the regular army, in connexion with the defection that has so considerably diminished the number of its officers, gives peculiar importance to his recommendation for increasing the corps of cadets to the greatest capacity of the Military Academy.

By mere omission, I presume, Congress has failed to provide chaplains for hospitals occupied by volunteers. This subject was brought to my notice, and I was induced to draw up the form of a letter, one copy of which, properly addressed, has been delivered to each of the persons, and at the dates respectively named and stated, in a schedule, containing also the form of the letter, marked A, and herewith transmitted.

These gentlemen, I understand, entered upon the duties designated, at the times respectively stated in the schedule, and have labored faithfully therein ever since. I therefore recommend that they be compensated at the same rate as chaplains in the army. I further suggest that general provision be made for chaplains to serve at hospitals, as well as with regiments.

The report of the Secretary of the Navy presents in detail the operations of that branch of the service, the activity and energy which have characterized its administration, and the results of measures to increase its efficiency and power. Such have been the additions, by construction and purchase, that it may almost be said a navy has been created and brought into service since our difficulties commenced.

Besides blockading our extensive coast, squadrons larger than ever before assembled under our flag have been put afloat and performed deeds which have increased our naval renown.

I would invite special attention to the recommendation of the Secretary for a more perfect organization of the navy by introducing additional grades in the service.

The present organization is defective and unsatisfactory, and the suggestions submitted by the department will, it is believed, if adopted, obviate the difficulties alluded to, promote harmony, and increase the efficiency of the navy.

There are three vacancies on the bench of the Supreme Court—two by the decease of Justices Daniel and McLean, and one by the resignation of Justice Campbell. I have so far forborne making nominations to fill these vacancies for reasons which I will now state. Two of the outgoing judges resided within the States now overrun by revolt; so that if successors were appointed in the same localities, they could not now serve upon their circuits; and many of the most competent men there, probably would not take the personal hazard of accepting to serve, even here, upon the supreme bench. I have been unwilling to throw all the appointments northward, thus disabling myself from doing justice to the south on the return of peace; although I may remark that to transfer to the north one which has heretofore been in the south, would not, with reference to territory and population, be unjust.

During the long and brilliant judicial career of Judge McLean his circuit grew into an empire—altogether too large for any one judge to give the courts therein more than a nominal attendance—rising in population from one million four hundred and seventy thousand and eighteen, in 1830, to six million one hundred and fifty-one thousand four hundred and five, in 1860.

Besides this, the country generally has outgrown our present judicial system. If uniformity was at all intended, the system requires that all the States shall be accommodated with circuit courts, attended by supreme judges, while, in fact, Wisconsin, Minnesota, Iowa, Kansas, Florida, Texas, California, and Oregon, have never had any such courts. Nor can this well be remedied without a change of the system; because the adding of judges to the Supreme Court, enough for the accommodation of all parts of the country, with circuit courts, would create a court altogether too numerous for a judicial body of any sort. And the evil, if it be one, will increase as new States come into the Union. Circuit courts are useful, or they are not useful. If useful, no State should be denied them ; if not useful, no State should have them. Let them be provided for all, or abolished as to all.

Three modifications occur to me, either of which, I think, would be an improvement upon our present system. Let the Supreme Court be of convenient number in every event. Then, first, let the whole country be divided into circuits of convenient size, the supreme judges to serve in a number of them corresponding to their own number, and independent circuit judges be provided for all the rest. Or, secondly, let the supreme judges be relieved from circuit duties, and circuit judges provided for all the circuits. Or, thirdly, dispense with circuit courts altogether, leaving the judicial functions wholly to the district courts and an independent Supreme Court.

I respectfully recommend to the consideration of Congress the present condition of the statute laws, with the hope that Congress will be able to find an easy remedy for many of the inconveniences and evils which constantly embarrass those engaged in the practical administration of them. Since the organization of the government, Congress has enacted some five thousand acts and joint resolutions, which fill more than six thousand closely printed pages, and are scattered through many volumes. Many of these acts have been drawn in haste and without sufficient caution, so that their provisions are often obscure in themselves, or in conflict with each other, or at least so doubtful as to render it very difficult for even the best informed persons to ascertain precisely what the statute law really is.

It seems to me very important that the statute laws should be made as plain and intelligible as possible, and be reduced to as small a compass as may consist with the fullness and precision of the will of the legislature and the perspicuity of its language. This, well done, would, I think, greatly facilitate the labors of those whose duty it is to assist in the administration of the laws, and would be a lasting benefit to the people, by placing before them, in a more accessible and intelligible form, the laws which so deeply concern their interests and their duties.

I am informed by some whose opinions I respect, that all the acts of Congress now in force, and of a permanent and general nature, might be revised and re-written, so as to be embraced in one volume (or at most, two volumes) of ordinary and convenient size. And I respectfully recommend to Congress to consider of the subject, and, if my suggestion be approved, to devise such plan as to their wisdom shall seem most proper for the attainment of the end proposed.

One of the unavoidable consequences of the present insurrection is the entire suppression, in many places, of all the ordinary means of administering civil justice by the officers, and in the forms of existing law. This is the case, in whole or in part, in all the insurgent States; and as our armies advance upon and take possession of parts of those States, the practical evil becomes more apparent. There are no courts nor officers to whom the citizens of other States may apply for the enforcement of their lawful claims against citizens of the insurgent States; and there is a vast amount of debt constituting such claims. Some have estimated it as high as two hundred million dollars, due, in large part, from insurgents, in open rebellion, to loyal citizens who are, even now, making great sacrifices in the discharge of their patriotic duty to support the government.

Under these circumstances, I have been urgently solicited to establish, by military power, courts to administer summary justice in such cases. I have thus far declined to do it, not because I had any doubt that the end proposed—the collection of the debts—was just and right in itself, but because I have been unwilling to go beyond the pressure of necessity in the unusual exercise of power. But the powers of Congress I suppose are equal to the anomalous occasion, and therefore I refer the whole matter to Congress, with the hope that a plan may be devised for the administration of justice in all such parts of the insurgent States and Territories as may be under the control of this government, whether by a voluntary return to allegiance and order, or by the power of our arms. This, however, not to be a permanent institution, but a temporary substitute, and to cease as soon as the ordinary courts can be re-established in peace.

It is important that some more convenient means should be provided, if possible, for the adjustment of claims against the government, especially in view of their increased number by reason of the war. It is as much the duty of government to render prompt justice against itself, in favor of citizens, as it is to administer the same, between private individuals. The investigation and adjudication of claims, in their nature belong to the judicial department ; besides it is apparent that the attention of Congress, will be more than usually engaged, for some time to come, with great national questions. It was intended, by the organization of the court of claims, mainly to remove this branch of business from the halls of Congress ; but while the court has proved to be an effective, and valuable means of investigation, it in great degree fails to effect the object of its creation, for want of power to make its judgments final.

Fully aware of the delicacy, not to say the danger, of the subject, I commend to your careful consideration whether this power of making judgments final, may not properly be given to the court, reserving the right of appeal on questions of law to the Supreme Court, with such other provisions as experience may have shown to be necessary.

I ask attention to the report of the Postmaster General, the following being a summary statement of the condition of the department:

The revenue from all sources during the fiscal year ending June 30, 1861, including the annual permanent appropriation of seven hundred thousand dollars for the transportation of ''free mail matter,'' was nine million forty-nine thousand two hundred and ninety-six dollars and forty cents, being about two per cent. less than the revenue for 1860.

The expenditures were thirteen million six hundred and six thousand seven hundred and fifty-nine dollars and eleven cents, showing a decrease of more than eight per cent. as compared with those of the previous year, and leaving an excess of expenditure over the revenue for the last fiscal year of four million five hundred and fifty-seven thousand four hundred and sixty-two dollars and seventy-one cents.

The gross revenue for the year ending June 30, 1863, is estimated at an increase of four per cent. on that of 1861, making eight million six hundred and eighty-three thousand dollars, to which should be added the earnings of the department in carrying free matter, viz: seven hundred thousand dollars, making nine million three hundred and eighty-three thousand dollars.

The total expenditures for 1863 are estimated at twelve million five hundred and twenty-eight thousand dollars, leaving an estimated deficiency of three million one hundred and forty-five thousand dollars to be supplied from the treasury, in addition to the permanent appropriation.

The present insurrection shows, I think, that the extension of this District across the Potomac river, at the time of establishing the capital here, was eminently wise, and consequently that the relinquishment of that portion of it which lies within the State of Virginia was unwise and dangerous. I submit for your consideration the expediency of regaining that part of the District, and the restoration of the original boundaries thereof, through negotiations with the State of Virginia.

The report of the Secretary of the Interior, with the accompanying documents, exhibits the condition of the several branches of the public business pertaining to that department. The depressing influences of the insurrection have been especially felt in the operations of the Patent and General Land Offices. The cash receipts from the sales of public lands during the past year have exceeded the expenses of our land system only about two hundred thousand dollars. The sales have been entirely suspended in the southern States, while the interruptions to the business of the country, and the diversion of large numbers of men from labor to military service, have obstructed settlements in the new States and Territories of the northwest.

The receipts of the Patent Office have declined in nine months about one hundred thousand dollars, rendering a large reduction of the force employed necessary to make it self-sustaining.

The demands upon the Pension Office will be largely increased by the insurrection. Numerous applications for pensions, based upon the casualties of the existing war, have already been made. There is reason to believe that many who are now upon the pension rolls and in receipt of the bounty of the government, are in the ranks of the insurgent army, or giving them aid and comfort. The Secretary of the Interior has directed a suspension of the payment of the pensions of such persons upon proof of their disloyalty. I recommend that Congress authorize that officer to cause the names of such persons to be stricken from the pension rolls.

The relations of the government with the Indian tribes have been greatly disturbed by the insurrection, especially in the southern superintendency and in that of New Mexico. The Indian country south of Kansas is in the possession of insurgents from Texas and Arkansas. The agents of the United States appointed since the 4th of March for this superintendency have been unable to reach their posts, while the most of those who were in office before that time have espoused the insurrectionary cause, and assume to exercise the powers of agents by virtue of commissions from the insurrectionists. It has been stated in the public press that a portion of those Indians have been organized as a military force, and are attached to the army of the insurgents. Although the government has no official information upon this subject, letters have been written to the Commissioner of Indian Affairs by several prominent chiefs, giving assurance of their loyalty to the United States, and expressing a wish for the presence of federal troops to protect them. It is believed that upon the repossession of the country by the federal forces the Indians will readily cease all hostile demonstrations, and resume their former relations to the government.   .

Agriculture, confessedly the largest interest of the nation, has, not a department, nor a bureau, but a clerkship only, assigned to it in the government. · While it is fortunate that this great interest is so independent in its nature as to not have demanded and extorted more from the government, I respectfully ask Congress to consider whether something more cannot be given voluntarily with general advantage.

Annual reports exhibiting the condition of our agriculture, commerce and manufactures would present a fund of information of great practical value to the country. While I make no suggestion as to details, I venture the opinion that an agricultural and statistical bureau might profitably be organized. '

The execution of the laws for the suppression of the African slave trade has been confided to the Department of the Interior. It is a subject of gratulation that the efforts which have been made for the suppression of this inhuman traffic have been recently attended with unusual success. Five vessels being fitted out for the slave trade have been seized and condemned. Two mates of vessels engaged in the trade, and one person in equipping a vessel as a slaver, have been convicted and subjected to the penalty of fine and imprisonment, and one captain, taken with a cargo of Africans on board his vessel, has been convicted of the highest grade of offence under our laws, the punishment of which is death.

The Territories of Colorado, Dakotah and Nevada, created by the last Congress, have been organized, and civil administration has been inaugurated therein under auspices especially gratifying, when it is considered that the leaven of treason was found existing in some of these new countries when the federal officers arrived there.

The abundant natural resources of these Territories, with the security and protection afforded by organized government, will doubtless invite to them a large immigration when peace shall restore the business of the country to its accustomed channels. I submit the resolutions of the legislature of Colorado, which evidence the patriotic spirit of the people of the Territory. So far the authority of the United States has been upheld in all the Territories, as it is hoped it will be in the future. I commend their interests and defence to the enlightened and generous care of Congress.

I recommend to the favorable consideration of Congress the interests of the District of Columbia. The insurrection has been the cause of much suffering and sacrifice to its inhabitants, and as they have no representative in Congress, that body should not overlook their just claims upon the government.

At your late session a joint resolution was adopted authorizing the President to take measures for facilitating a proper representation of the industrial interests of the United States at the exhibition of the industry of all nations to be holden at London in the year 1862. I regret to say I have been unable to give personal attention to this subject—a subject at once so interesting in itself, and so extensively and intimately connected with the material prosperity of the world. Through the Secretaries of State and of the Interior a plan, or system, has been devised, and partly matured, and which will be laid before you.

Under and by virtue of the act of Congress entitled "An act to confiscate property used for insurrectionary purposes," approved August 6, 1861, the legal claims of certain persons to the labor and service of certain other persons have become forfeited; and numbers of the latter, thus liberated, are already dependent on the United States, and must be provided for in some way. Besides this, it is not impossible that some of the States will pass similar enactments for their own benefit respectively, and by operation of which, persons of the same class will be thrown upon them for disposal. In such case I recommend that Congress provide for accepting such persons from such States, according to some mode of valuation, in lieu, *pro tanto*, of direct taxes, or upon some other plan to be agreed on with such States respectively ; that such persons, on such acceptance by the general government, be at once deemed free ; and that, in any event, steps be taken for colonizing both classes, (or the one first mentioned, if the other shall not be brought into existence,) at some place, or places, in a climate congenial to them. It might be well to consider, too, whether the free colored people already in the United States could not, so far as individuals may desire, be included in such colonization.

To carry out the plan of colonization may involve the acquiring of territory, and also the appropriation of money beyond that to be expended in the territorial acquisition. Having practiced the acquisition of territory for nearly sixty years, the question of constitutional power to do so is no longer an open one with us. The power was questioned at first by Mr. Jefferson, who, however, in the purchase of Louisiana, yielded his scruples on the plea of great expediency. If it be said that the only legitimate object of acquiring territory is to furnish homes for white men, this measure effects that object ; for the emigration of colored men leaves additional room for white men remaining or coming here. Mr. Jefferson, however, placed the importance of procuring Louisiana more on political and commercial grounds than on providing room for population.

On this whole proposition, including the appropriation of money with the acquisition of territory, does not the expediency amount to absolute necessity—that, without which the government itself cannot be perpetuated ?

The war continues. In considering the policy to be adopted for suppressing the insurrection, I have been anxious and careful that the inevitable conflict for this purpose shall not degenerate into a violent and remorseless revolutionary struggle. I have, therefore, in every case, thought it proper to keep the integrity of the Union prominent as the primary object of the contest on our part, leaving all questions which are not of vital military importance to the more deliberate action of the legislature.

In the exercise of my best discretion I have adhered to the blockade of the ports held by the insurgents, instead of putting in force, by proclamation, the law of Congress enacted at the late session for closing those ports.

So, also, obeying the dictates of prudence, as well as the obligations of law, instead of transcending, I have adhered to the act of

Congress to confiscate property used for insurrectionary purposes. If a new law upon the same subject shall be proposed, its propriety will be duly considered.   The Union must be preserved; and hence, all indispensable means must be employed.   We should not be in haste to determine that radical, and extreme measures, which may reach the loyal as well as the disloyal, are indispensable.

The inaugural address at the beginning of the Administration, and the message to Congress at the late special session, were both mainly devoted to the domestic controversy out of which the insurrection and consequent war have sprung.   Nothing now occurs to add or subtract, to or from, the principles, or general purposes, stated and expressed, in those documents.

The last ray of hope for preserving the Union peaceably, expired at the assault upon Fort Sumter; and a general review of what has occurred since may not be unprofitable.   What was painfully uncertain then, is much better defined and more distinct now; and the progress of events is plainly in the right direction. The insurgents confidently claimed a strong support from north of Mason and Dixon's line; and the friends of the Union were not free from apprehension on the point.   This, however, was soon settled definitely, and on the right side.   South of the line, noble little Delaware led off right from the first.   Maryland was made to *seem* against the Union.   Our soldiers were assaulted, bridges were burned, and railroads torn up, within her limits; and we were many days, at one time, without the ability to bring a single regiment over her soil to the capital.   Now, her bridges and railroads are repaired and open to the government; she already gives seven regiments to the cause of the Union and none to the enemy; and her people, at a regular election, have sustained the Union, by a larger majority, and a larger aggregate vote than they ever before gave to any candidate, or any question.   Kentucky, too, for some time in doubt, is now decidedly, and, I think, unchangeably, ranged on the side of the Union.   Missouri is comparatively quiet; and I believe cannot again be overrun by the insurrectionists.   These three States of Maryland, Kentucky, and Missouri, neither of which would promise a single soldier at first, have now an aggregate of not less than forty thousand in the field, for the Union; while, of their citizens, certainly not more than a third of that number, and they of doubtful whereabouts, and doubtful existence, are in arms against it.   After a somewhat bloody struggle of months, winter closes on the Union people of western Virginia, leaving them masters of their own country.

An insurgent force of about fifteen hundred, for months dominating the narrow peninsular region, constituting the counties of Accomac and Northampton, and known as eastern shore of Virginia, together with some contiguous parts of Maryland, have laid down their arms; and the people there have renewed their allegiance to, and accepted the protection of, the old flag. This leaves no armed insurrectionist north of the Potomac, or east of the Chesapeake.

Also we have obtained a footing at each of the isolated points, on the southern coast, of Hatteras, Port Royal, Tybee Island, near Savannah, and Ship island; and we likewise have some general accounts of popular movements, in behalf of the Union, in North Carolina and Tennessee.

These things demonstrate that the cause of the Union is advancing steadily and certainly southward.

Since your last adjournment, Lieutenant General Scott has retired from the head of the army. During his long life, the nation has not been unmindful of his merit; yet, on calling to mind how faithfully, ably, and brilliantly he has served the country, from a time far back in our history, when few of the now living had been born, and thenceforward continually, I cannot but think we are still his debtors. I submit, therefore, for your consideration, what further mark of recognition is due to him, and to ourselves, as a grateful people.

With the retirement of General Scott came the executive duty of appointing, in his stead, a general-in-chief of the army. It is a fortunate circumstance that neither in council nor country was there, so far as I know, any difference of opinion as to the proper person to be selected. The retiring chief repeatedly expressed his judgment in favor of General McClellan for the position; and in this the nation seemed to give a unanimous concurrence. The designation of General McClellan is, therefore, in considerable degree, the selection of the country, as well as of the Executive; and hence there is better reason to hope there will be given him, the confidence, and cordial support thus, by fair implication, promised, and without which, he cannot, with so full efficiency, serve the country.

It has been said that one bad general is better than two good ones; and the saying is true, if taken to mean no more than that an army is better directed by a single mind, though inferior, than by two superior ones, at variance, and cross-purposes with each other.

And the same is true, in all joint operations wherein those engaged, *can* have none but a common end in view, and *can* differ only as to the choice of means. In a storm at sea, no one on board *can* wish the ship to sink; and yet, not unfrequently, all go down together, because too many will direct, and no single mind can be allowed to control.

It continues to develop that the insurrection is largely, if not exclusively, a war upon the first principle of popular government—the rights of the people. Conclusive evidence of this is found in the most grave and maturely considered public documents, as well as in the general tone of the insurgents. In those documents we find the abridgment of the existing right of suffrage, and the denial to the people of all right to participate in the selection of public officers, except the legislative, boldly advocated, with labored arguments to prove that large control of the people in government, is the source of all political evil. Monarchy itself is sometimes hinted at as a possible refuge from the power of the people.

In my present position, I could scarcely be justified were I to omit raising a warning voice against this approach of returning despotism.

It is not needed, nor fitting here, that a general argument should be made in favor of popular institutions; but there is one point, with its connexions, not so hackneyed as most others, to which I ask a brief attention. It is the effort to place *capital* on an equal footing with, if not above *labor*, in the structure of government. It is assumed that labor is available only in connexion with capital; that nobody labors unless somebody else, owning capital, somehow by the use of it, induces him to labor. This assumed, it is next considered whether it is best that capital shall *hire* laborers, and thus induce them to work by their own consent, or *buy* them, and drive them to it without their consent. Having proceded so far, it is naturally concluded that all laborers are either *hired* laborers, or what we call slaves. And further, it is assumed that whoever is once a hired laborer, is fixed in that condition for life.

Now, there is no such relation between capital and labor as assumed; nor is there any such thing as a free man being fixed for life in the condition of a hired laborer.   Both these assumptions are false, and all inferences from them are groundless.

Labor is prior to, and independent of, capital.   Capital is only the fruit of labor, and could never have existed if labor had not first existed.   Labor is the superior of capital, and deserves much the higher consideration.   Capital has its rights, which are as worthy of protection as any other rights.   Nor is it denied that there is, and probably always will be, a relation between labor and capital, producing mutual benefits.   The error is in assuming that the whole labor of community exists within that relation.   A few men own capital, and that few avoid labor themselves, and, with their capital, hire or buy another few to labor for them.   A large majority belong to neither class—neither work for others, nor have others working for them.   In most of the southern States, a majority of the whole people of all colors, are neither slaves nor masters; while in the northern, a large majority are neither hirers nor hired.   Men with their families—wives, sons, and daughters—work for themselves, on their farms, in their houses, and in their shops, taking the whole product to themselves, and asking no favors of capital on the one hand, nor of hired laborers or slaves on the other.   It is not forgotten that a considerable number of persons mingle their own labor with capital—that is, they labor with their own hands, and also buy or hire others to labor for them; but this is only a mixed, and not a distinct class.   No principle stated is disturbed by the existence of this mixed class.

Again: as has already been said, there is not, of necessity, any such thing as the free hired laborer being fixed to that condition for life.   Many independent men everywhere in these States, a few years back in their lives, were hired laborers.   The prudent, penniless beginner in the world, labors for wages awhile, saves a surplus with which to buy tools or land for himself; then labors on his own account another while, and at length hires another new beginner to help him.   This is the just, and generous, and prosperous system, which opens the way to all—gives hope to all, and consequent energy, and progress, and improvement of condition to all.   No men living are more worthy to be trusted than those who toil up from poverty—none less inclined to take, or touch, aught which they have not honestly earned.   Let them beware of surrendering a political power which they already possess, and which, if surrendered, will surely be used to close the door of advancement against such as they, and to fix new disabilities and burdens upon them, till all of liberty shall be lost.

From the first taking of our National Census to the last, are seventy years; and we find our population, at the end of the period, eight times as great as it was at the beginning. The increase of those other things, which men deem desirable, has been even greater. We thus have, at one view, what the popular principle, applied to government, through the machinery of the States and the Union, has produced in a given time; and also what, if firmly maintained, it promises for the future. There are already among us those who, if the Union be preserved, will live to see it contain two hundred and fifty millions. The struggle *of* to-day is not altogether *for* to-day— it is for a vast future also. With a reliance on Providence, all the more firm and earnest, let us proceed in the great task which events have devolved upon us.

                                        ABRAHAM LINCOLN.

Washington, *December* 3, 1861.

Schedule A.

                                        EXECUTIVE MANSION,
                    Washington, D. C.,   1861.

Rev. ———— ————.

Sir: Having been solicited by Christian ministers, and other pious people, to appoint suitable persons to act as chaplains at the hospitals for our sick and wounded soldiers, and feeling the intrinsic propriety of having such persons to so act, and yet believing there is no law conferring the power upon me to appoint them, I think fit to say that if you will voluntarily enter upon and perform the appropriate duties of such position, I will recommend that Congress make compensation therefor at the same rate as chaplains in the army are compensated.

The following are the names and dates, respectively, of the persons and times to whom and when such letters were delivered:

Rev. G. G. Goss	September 25, 1861.
Rev. John G. Butler	September 25, 1861.
Rev. Henry Hopkins	September 25, 1861.
Rev. F. M. Magrath	October 30, 1861.
Rev. F. E. Boyle	October 30, 1861.
Rev. John C. Smith	November 7, 1861.
Rev. Wm. Y. Brown	November 7, 1861.

REPORT

OF

THE SECRETARY OF THE INTERIOR.

DEPARTMENT OF THE INTERIOR, *November* 30, 1861.

SIR: The report of the operations of this department during the fiscal year ending June 30, 1861, will exhibit a diminished amount of business in some of the most important bureaus connected with the department. This is attributable mainly to the insurrection which has suddenly precipitated the country into a civil war.

GENERAL LAND OFFICE.

The decline of business has very sensibly affected the operations of the General Land Office. Official intercourse has been entirely suspended with all the southern States which contain any portion of the public lands, and consequently no sales have been made in any of those States.

In all the northern States in which any of the public lands are situated the war has almost entirely suspended sales. The demand for volunteers has called into the ranks of the army a large number of that portion of our people whose energy and enterprise in time of peace incline them to emigrate to the west and settle upon the public lands, thus laying the foundations of future prosperous communities and States. Besides, the ordinary channels of trade and commerce have been so obstructed by the war that the sources of income, from which the settlers upon the public lands have realized the means of purchasing, have been greatly diminished.

On the 30th September, 1861, there were 55,555,595.25 acres of the public lands which had been surveyed but not proclaimed for public sale. The lands surveyed and offered at public sale previous to that time, and then subject to private entry, amounted to 78,662,735.64 acres, making an aggregate of public lands surveyed and ready for sale of 134,218,330.89 acres.

Since the last annual report of this department no proclamation for a public sale of lands has been made, as the quantity already subject to private entry is more than sufficient to meet the wants of the country. During the fiscal year ending 30th June, 1861, and the first quarter of the current year, ending 30th September, 1861, 5,289,532.31 acres have been disposed of. Of this amount 1,021,493.77 acres have been certified to the States of Minnesota, Michigan, and Louisiana, under railroad grants made by Congress; 606,094.47 acres have been certified to States as swamp lands; 2,153.940 acres have been located with bounty land warrants, and 1,508,004.07 acres have been sold for cash, producing $925,299 42.

It will be seen from this statement that the public lands have ceased substantially for the present, at least, to be a source of revenue to the government. The liberal manner in which the acts of Congress, granting swamp and overflowed lands to the States, have been construed and executed, the grants of large quantities to aid in the construction of railroads, and the quantity required to locate bounty land warrants for military services, have combined to reduce the cash sales to an amount but little more than sufficient to meet the expenses of our land system. The net income from sales during the last fiscal year will hardly reach the sum of $200,000. During the last fiscal year there were certified to the States for railroad construction, under the several acts of Congress making grants for such purposes: To Minnesota, 308,871.90 acres; to Michigan, 636,061.42 acres; and to Louisiana, 76,560.45 acres. The whole amount certified to all the States, under such grants, is 9,998,497.77 acres.

The grants of swamp and overflowed lands to the States have absorbed a large amount of valuable lands, and have caused a heavy drain upon the treasury. The claims of the several States cover an aggregate of 57,895,577.40 acres.

The United States have also paid to the States, in cash, under the indemnity act of March 2, 1855, on account of lands claimed as swamp lands, and which were sold by the United States subsequent to the date of the grant, $276,126 50.

Certificates have been issued for location upon any of the public lands subject to entry, to indemnify the States for lands claimed as swamp lands, but which had been located by bounty land warrants after the date of the grant, amounting to 145,595.92 acres. Additional claims are pending, yet undecided, for cash, $142,435, and for lands, 301,429 acres.

The bounty land warrants and scrip issued under different acts of Congress, previous to September 30, 1861, embrace an aggregate of 71,717,172 acres of land. Of this amount there have been located: For revolutionary services, 8,200,612 acres; for services in the war with Great Britain, 4,850,120 acres; for Canadian volunteers, 72,750 acres; for services in the Mexican war and other services, under the acts of 1847, 1850, 1852, and 1855, in all 51,138,970 acres; leaving yet to be located on warrants and scrip, already issued, 7,454,720 acres.

Unless Congress shall authorize the issue of additional warrants, this drain upon the public lands will soon cease.

The propriety of issuing bounty land warrants to the volunteers who have been called into service to suppress the existing insurrection, is already a subject of discussion, and must be determined by Congress. A warrant for 160 acres to each volunteer engaged in the service would absorb over one hundred millions of acres, a much larger amount than has been issued under all previous laws. It is evident that the issue of such an amount of warrants would destroy all hope of deriving any revenue from the public lands, at least for many years. And while such a measure would deprive the government of all income from this source, it would afford but little benefit to the volunteers. These warrants are now sold in the market at about fifty cents per acre. An addition of the large amount necessary to supply the volunteers would necessarily reduce the price of them to a merely nominal sum.

The bounty of the government, dispensed to the volunteers in this form, would fail to realize to them the advantages intended. All the best lands would fall into the hands of speculators, who would be enabled to purchase them at a nominal price and sell them to settlers at full prices as fast as emigration to the west would require them for settlement. If additional compensation to the volunteers, beyond the amount now authorized by law, shall be deemed just and proper, it will be better both for the government and the volunteers to make such compensation by a direct appropriation of money, or of government securities. This would give them the full benefit of the appropriations made, while the government would, by keeping the lands until they shall be demanded for settlement, realize their full value.

The expense of surveying private land claims in the territory acquired from Mexico, based upon grants of the Mexican government, have heretofore been paid by the United States. These surveys have cost the government large sums. The cost of surveying one claim amounted to twenty-two hundred dollars; another cost the government fourteen hundred dollars. The aggregate cost of surveying them has taken from the treasury a large amount of the public funds. No valid reason exists, in my judgment, for taxing the government with the cost of these surveys. There is no obligation resting upon the United States to ascertain and define the boundaries of grants made by Mexico to individuals previous to the cession of the territory. The claimant realizes all the benefit and should be charged with the expenses of defining the boundary of his claim. The surveys should be made under the authority of the United States, but the cost of the survey should be paid by the claimants, and patents for the land should be withheld until the expenses of the survey are paid.

The valuable and extensive mineral lands owned by the government in California and New Mexico have hitherto produced no revenue. All who chose to do so have been permitted to work them without limitation. It is believed that no other government owning valuable mineral lands has ever refused to avail itself of the opportunity of deriving a revenue from the privilege of mining such lands. They are the property of the whole people, and it would be obviously just and proper to require those who reap the advantages of mining them to pay a reasonable amount as a consideration for the advantages enjoyed.

The territorial governments of Colorado, Dakotah, and Nevada have been successfully organized since the adjournment of the last Congress. The surveys of the public lands in those Territories have already been commenced, and the lands are now open for settlement. The productiveness of the soil and the mineral wealth of those Territories, with· the advantages of legally organized governments, will doubtless invite a large immigration to them as soon as the termination of the war shall restore to civil employments that portion of our people now under arms.

Congress, by an act passed May 26, 1860, authorized the appointment by the President "of a suitable person or persons" who should, in conjunction with persons to be appointed on behalf of the State of California, "run and mark the boundary lines between the Territories of the United States and the State of California." Fifty-five thousand dollars was appropriated for the performance of the work. Sylvester Mowry was appointed a commissioner on the part of the United States, and the sum of $37,551 19 was placed at his disposal for the prosecution of the work.

Very soon after taking charge of the department, I ascertained that the whole sum which had been placed in the hands of the commissioner had been disposed of by him, and a large amount of drafts for additional sums had been drawn upon the department, while no progress had been made in the work beyond the fixing of one of three initial points, viz: the intersection of the 35th parallel of north latitude with the Colorado river. The whole appropriation had been squandered, while the work had been only commenced. Under these circumstances I deemed it to be my duty to arrest the creation of further claims against the government without authority of law, and accordingly directed the suspension of the work and a discontinuance of the services of the commissioner. It is believed that the whole work might have been completed for the sum appropriated by Congress; but while only a small part of the work has been accomplished, the claims presented amount to nearly $20,000 beyond the appropriation. It remains for Congress to determine whether further appropriations shall be made for the continuance of the work.

The running of the boundary lines between the Territories of the United States and the State of Texas, authorized by the act of Congress of June 5, 1858, has been completed in the field, and the office details will in a short time be finished. For this work $80,000 was appropriated. Of this sum $73,250 81 had been expended on the 30th September, 1861, leaving an unexpended balance of $6,749 19. This balance is estimated to be sufficient for the completion of the entire work.

For more detailed information in regard to the operations of the General Land Office, reference is made to the able and elaborate report of the Commissioner.

INDIAN AFFAIRS.

Our Indian affairs are in a very unsettled and unsatisfactory condition.

The spirit of rebellion against the authority of the government, which has precipitated a large number of States into open revolt, has been instilled into a portion of the Indian tribes by emissaries from the insurrectionary States.

The large tribes of Cherokees, Chickasaws, and Choctaws, situated in the southern superintendency, have suspended all intercourse with the agents of the United States.

The superintendent and agents appointed since the 4th of March last have been unable to reach their posts or to hold any intercourse with the tribes under their charge. The superintendent and some, if not all, of the agents of the southern superintendency, who were in office on the 4th of March, have assumed an attitude of revolt to the United States, and have instigated the Indians to acts of hostility. Some of these, who lately held their offices under the United States, now claim to exercise the same authority by virtue of commissions from the pretended confederate government.

Although the Indian Office has not been able to procure definite information of the condition of affairs, and of the extent to which the Indians have assumed a hostile attitude, enough has been ascertained to leave no room for doubt that the influences which have been exerted upon the Indians have been sufficient to induce a portion of them to renounce the authority of the United States and to acknowledge that of the rebel government.

It has been currently reported through the press that a portion of them have been organized as a military force, and are in arms with the rebels; but the department has no official information confirming these rumors.

The hostile attitude assumed by portions of the tribes referred to, has resulted from their fears, produced by violence and threats of emissaries sent among them, and the withdrawal from their vicinity of the troops of the United States, whose presence would have afforded a guarantee of protection. It is unfortunate that the War Department has been unable to send to that region such a body of troops as would be adequate to the protection of those tribes, and revive their confidence in the ability as well as the will of the United States to comply with their treaty stipulations. Cut off from all intercourse with loyal citizens ; surrounded by emissaries from the rebels, who represented that the government of the United States was destroyed, and who promised that the rebel government would assume the obligations of the United States and pay their annuities; assailed by threats of violence, and seeing around them no evidence of the power of the United States to protect them, it is not surprising that their loyalty was unable to resist such influences. Many white men of far greater intelligence have joined the insurrectionists against their own convictions of right, under much less pressure.

We have reason to believe that as soon as the United States shall re-establish their authority in the Indian country, and shall send there a sufficient force for the protection of the tribes, they will renounce all connexion with the rebel government and resume their former relations with the United States.

The payment of their annuities has been suspended. The Commissioner of Indian Affairs expresses the opinion, in which I concur, that Congress should make the usual appropriations to comply with the treaty stipulations of the United States, that the means may exist to pay them, if circumstances and the condition of the tribes shall hereafter render it proper and expedient to do so.

The tribes upon the Pacific slope of the Rocky mountains have manifested a turbulent spirit, but have committed no acts of violence. With vigilance on the part of the agents it is hoped they may be restrained from depredations upon the white settlers, and be gradually brought under the control of the laws of the United States.

Much trouble has been experienced in New Mexico from depredations committed by some of the tribes in that Territory. The withdrawal of the troops of the United States has encouraged them to acts of violence, while the active interference of disloyal persons from Texas has induced them to disregard the laws and authority of the government. The presence of a military force in that Territory is indispensable to preserve the peace and cause the Indians to respect the laws.

The tribes in Kansas and Nebraska, and in the States of the northwest, are gradually progressing in the arts of civilization. The plan of allotting portions of their reservations to the individual members of the tribes has been found by experience to result beneficially. Many of them have improved their lands and become quite proficient as farmers. A continuance of this policy, by familiarizing them with the habits of agricultural life, will gradually lead them to depend upon the cultivation of the soil for subsistence.

The report of the Commissioner of Indian Affairs, which is herewith submitted, furnishes full information in regard to the several tribes, and suggests in detail such matters as require the action of Congress.

The practice of licensing traders to traffic with the Indians, has been productive of mischievous results. The money received by them in payment of their annuities, generally passes immediately into the hands of the traders. The Indians purchase goods of the traders upon a credit, to be paid for upon the receipt of their next annuity. When the payment is due, the debts of the Indians are usually sufficient to absorb the whole amount. But, if anything is left after the payment of their debts, it is used for new purchases from the traders. The result of this system of trade is that the Indians pay for the goods they purchase, much more than they are worth. But this is not the only evil resulting from it. When a treaty is made, a large array of debts is presented, and provision usually made in the treaty for their payment. Witnesses are produced who establish the debts by evidence, which cannot be contradicted by any available proof, sufficient to absorb most of the proceeds of their lands. They are left to depend upon their annuities from the government for subsistence, and these find their way into the hands of the traders, while the Indians receive from them goods at a profit of from one to three or four hundred per cent.

It is apparent to all acquainted with Indians, that they are incompetent to manage their own business, or to protect their rights in their intercourse with the white race. It is the duty of the government to shield them from the arts of designing men, and to see that they realize the full benefit of the annuities to which they are entitled. This can only be accomplished by breaking up the whole system of Indian trading. The power granted to agents to license persons to trade with the Indians should be revoked. All contracts made with them, and all obligations for goods or other property sold to them, should be declared utterly void. All future treaties should provide for the payment of their annuities in goods and agricultural implements, at the lowest prices at which they can be procured by the government. The department should be authorized to procure the consent of the tribes, with which treaties exist providing for the payment of cash annuities, that it shall furnish them with such goods and agricultural implements as their wants require, at the wholesale prices of such articles in the best markets, in lieu of the cash annuities provided for in the treaties.

By such a change the Indians would avoid the payment of profits which are now paid to the traders, and would realize a much larger amount in goods for their annuities than they now receive.

PATENT OFFICE.

No branch of the public service connected with this department has been so much affected by the insurrection of the southern States as that of the Patent Office.

The receipts of the office from January 1 to September 30, 1861, were $102,808 18; and the expenditures were $185,594 05, showing an excess of expenditures over receipts of $82,785 87.

During the corresponding period of the last year the receipts were $197,348 40, being $94,840 22 more than the receipts for the same part of this year. During the same period 3,514 applications for patents and 519 caveats have been filed, 2,581 patents have been issued, and 15 patents have been extended.

To meet this deficiency in the income of the office, the commissioner, with the concurrence of the department, has reduced the clerical and examining force by the discharge of thirty of the employés, and reduced the grade of the remainder in order to lessen their compensation. By this reduction it is believed by the commissioner that the expenditures will be brought within the receipts.

The expenses of the office have been increased during the present year by the printing of the drawings and specifications authorized by the 14th section of the act of March 2, 1861. The Commissioner contracted for the printing in conformity with the law, and the work was executed in a satisfactory manner until the 1st of November, when, in consequence of the decline in the receipts of the office, it was discontinued.

The printing of the drawings and specifications of patents, in the manner in which it has been done under the law of March last, would unquestionably be of great service to the office, as well as to all interested in its business, and should, if possible, be continued. Although the expenses of the Patent Office have been increased by this printing, a saving of a larger amount has been effected to the treasury. The mechanical reports of the Patent Office have heretofore been printed at the expense of the government. These reports consist of extracts from the specifications of the patents issued, giving a brief and general description of the improvements or inventions for which the patents were issued. They possess no interest for the general reader, while they are too brief to be of service to mechanics or inventors. The plates for the Mechanical Report of 1860 cost the government $47,398 21—a sum greater than the entire cost of printing provided for by the law of March last. The cost of paper, printing, and binding was probably as much more, while the work was without practical value. The printing of the drawings and specifications, as provided for by the law of March last, will render unnecessary the printing the mechanical reports, and save the expense heretofore incurred for their publication.

Several amendments to the law of March last are proposed by the Commissioner of Patents, which would doubtless render it more effective, and they are recommended to the favorable consideration of Congress.

The law regulating copy-rights should be amended to effect the objects contemplated by Congress.

The act of February 3, 1851, authorizes the clerks of the United States district courts to grant copy-rights, and requires the author to deposit a copy of his work with the clerk. The clerks are required to send to the Department of the Interior all such copies deposited in their offices. This duty is very imperfectly performed. Probably not more than half the books, maps, charts, and musical compositions which are copy-righted are deposited in this department, as required by law.

The object of collecting in one library copies of all the copy-righted literary productions of the country is thus defeated. To secure this object an amendment of the law is recommended which shall give the sole power of granting copy-rights to the Commissioner of Patents, and require from every applicant the payment of a fee of one dollar and a deposit in the Patent Office of a copy of the work to be copy-righted.

PENSION OFFICE.

The report of the Commissioner of Pensions furnishes, in detail, the operations of this bureau during the past year. The number of pensions has diminished, during the year, five hundred and seventy-five, and the amount required to pay them was $43,246 87 less than the previous year.

The whole number of pensioners, of all classes, on the rolls on the 30th of June, 1861, was 10,709, requiring for their payment an aggregate of $957,772 08.

They were classified as follows: 4,725 invalid pensioners, receiving $425,256 02; 63 revolutionary pensioners, receiving $3,690 85; 2,728 widows of revolutionary soldiers, receiving $212,548 36; 2,236 widows and orphans, half-pay, receiving $178,672; 957 navy pensioners, receiving $137,604 85.

The casualties of the conflict in which the government is now engaged, will increase the list of pensioners very largely. The amount of the increase cannot be estimated, as it will depend upon the duration of the war. The large amount of business which will necessarily be thrown upon the office from this cause will render an increase of the clerical force employed indispensable.

The Commissioner of Pensions, with the concurrence of the department, has construed the pension laws now in force as authorizing the granting of pensions to invalids and the widows and children of deceased soldiers who have been killed or wounded in the existing insurrection. If this construction of the laws should be deemed improper, the corrective is with Congress.

It has been ascertained that many of those who have been placed upon the pension rolls in the insurrectionary States have attached themselves to the rebel cause, and have taken up arms against the government. I have deemed it my duty in all such cases to direct a suspension of the payment of the pensions awarded to them. I have also directed a suspension of payment to all pensioners in any of the States who have in any manner encouraged the rebels, or manifested a sympathy with their cause.

It is respectfully suggested that Congress should authorize this department to cause the names of all such persons to be stricken from the pension rolls.

EIGHTH CENSUS.

The returns of the Eighth Census are being condensed for publication, with all the expedition practicable in a work of such magnitude and varied and comprehensive details.

The report which the Superintendent of that work will be prepared to make during the present Congress, will confirm the general belief, that no previous period of our history has been distinguished by greater prosperity or evidences of more substantial progress in all the material interests effecting the welfare and happiness of a people.

In this connexion I feel constrained to recommend the establishment of a Bureau of Agriculture and Statistics, the need whereof is not only realized by the heads of department, but is felt by every intelligent legislator.

The maintenance of such a bureau, on a respectable footing, by a different arrangement of offices which at present exist on a basis too contracted for extensive usefulness, would be attended with no expense to the government additional to that incident to the present organization of the departments, while the advantages gained to the public service would be incalculable. One of the objects contemplated by Congress in the appropriations for the promotion of agriculture was the "collection of agricultural statistics." Correct reports from every portion of the country exhibiting the peculiarities of the soils and their adaptation to the various crops, with the character and extent of their annual productions, would constitute a fund of information of great practical value. The appropriations heretofore made by Congress have not been sufficient to accomplish this object, and at the same time provide for the distribution of seeds and the propagation of new varieties of plants to the extent which the public expectation appeared to demand.

Annual reports made under the direction of such a bureau, setting forth the condition of our agriculture, manufactures, and commerce, with well digested statements relative to similar facts in foreign countries, which the present rapid intercommunication enables us to obtain often in advance of their publication abroad, would prove the most valuable repertories of interesting and important information, the absence of which often occasions incalculable loss to the material interests of the country. The vigilance of such a bureau would supply timely warning of the failure of crops abroad or at home, and lead to the judicious investment of capital and employment of labor in agriculture and manufactures.

While we expend vast sums for experiments in gunnery—the promotion of science—in illustrating the physical features of unpeopled territory at home and regions beyond the seas, and publish costly volumes of undigested correspondence relating to foreign trade, it is a source of pain to every statesman and political economist to reflect that it is only once in ten years that the country is supplied with reliable returns respecting the value of our agriculture and manufactures, while altogether ignorant of the extent of our internal commerce and possess no means of ascertaining its importance.

All enlightened foreign governments and several of the States sustain statistical bureaus, while the United States, with a population second to no other in intelligence, and with productions and resources the most varied, have yet to institute an agency which would prove an invaluable guardian of our most material interests. The want of such a bureau has long been felt and has been frequently brought to the notice of Congress, but at no period has the necessity been so universally recognized as at the present.

Upon the Agricultural and Statistical Bureau would naturally devolve the charge of the census, for which timely preparation would be made, and its administration conducted with improved accuracy and ease. In fact the execution of that work collects a mass of valuable details, and reveals innumerable and reliable sources of information of deep interest, heretofore lost to the country, which a permanent bureau would be able to develope to advantage.

The extent to which the documents of that office have reached, and the frequent reference made to them for public and private purposes, make it indispensable to maintain a permanent clerical force to have them in charge. Confident that such a bureau will assert its claim to public preservation, and by its utility prove the wisdom of he measure, I recommend its immediate formation.

AFRICAN SLAVE TRADE.

The President, by an order dated the 2d of May last, devolved upon this department the execution of the act of 3d March, 1819, and other laws enacted for the suppression of the African slave trade.

The subject was immediately taken in hand, under a deep sense of our obligation as a nation, to put an end, if possible, to this odious traffic, and with a full conviction that the power of the government, in the hands of competent, honest, and faithful officers, was adequate to the purpose. Among other things, I caused the marshals of the loyal Atlantic States to assemble at New York for consultation, in order to insure greater concert of action. They were thereby afforded an opportunity of inspecting vessels fully equipped for the African slave trade, and of seeing the arts and devices employed to disguise and conceal the real objects of their voyage, thus enabling them to detect and prevent the clearance of vessels designed for this trade. It is gratifying to know that unprecedented success has crowned the efforts of the past few months. Five vessels have been seized, tried, and condemned by the courts. One slaver has been taken on the coast of Africa with about nine hundred negroes on board, who were conveyed to the republic of Liberia. One person has been convicted at New York as the captain of a slaver, having on board eight hundred captives, and two others, (mates of a different vessel,) and another one at Boston for fitting out a vessel for the slave trade. In the first named case the penalty is death; in the others it is fine and imprisonment. Hitherto convictions under the laws prohibiting the African slave trade have been very rare.

This is probably the largest number ever obtained, and certainly the only ones for many years. It is believed that the first mentioned case is the only one involving capital punishment in which a conviction has been effected.

The full execution of the law in these instances will no doubt have a most salutary influence in deterring others from the commission of like offences.

A number of other indictments have been found which are yet to be tried.

Much credit is due to the United States attorneys and marshals at New York and Boston for the vigilance and zeal evinced by them, and I avail myself of the first occasion to make them this public acknowledgement.

Within a little more than a year the government of the United States, under contracts made with the government of Liberia, through the agency of the American Colonization Society, have taken into that republic four thousand five hundred Africans, recaptured on the high seas by vessels of our navy. They are supplied with food, clothing, and shelter, medicines and medical attendance, for one year from the date of landing, and are thus brought within the civilizing and christianizing influences of a government founded and administered by intelligent and right-minded persons of their own race.

They are under the special charge and supervision of an agent of the United States, the Rev. John Seys, who has been a devoted missionary in Africa for many years. His report, when received, will no doubt afford abundant evidence of the wisdom and philanthropy of the policy adopted by the United States in regard to these unhappy victims of a cruel and relentless cupidity, whose misfortunes have thrown them upon the fostering care and protection of the American people.

Great Britain and the United States have engaged, by the treaty dated at Washington the 9th of August, 1842, that each shall prepare, equip, and maintain in service on the coast of Africa a sufficient and adequate squadron or naval force of vessels of suitable numbers and descriptions, to carry in all not less than eighty guns, to enforce, separately and respectively, the laws, rights, and obligations of each of the two countries for the suppression of the slave trade.

It seems to be the opinion of those having most experience on the subject, that two or three fast steam vessels-of-war stationed on the coast of Africa would be able (in consequence of the light winds that usually prevail there and their capacity to go in any direction) to more effectually accomplish the object than a much larger number of sailing vessels.   Vessels are always selected for the slave trade with special reference to their sailing qualities; and it would probably be wise to seek a modification of the treaty of 1842, in order to admit of some such change in the character of the vessels employed.

But, after all, while we must continue to watch the coast of Africa, the most economical and effectual mode of preventing our citizens from engaging in the slave trade is by preventing the fitting out of vessels in our own waters for that purpose, and the plans now in operation will therefore continue to be vigorously prosecuted.

It is believed that the unexpended balances of appropriations for the suppression of the slave trade will be sufficient to meet the requirements of the service during the next fiscal year, and no further appropriation is asked; but that fact will render it necessary to remove the limitation in the appropriation of March 2, 1861, as to the compensation that may be allowed to marshals and others who may be employed.   The limitation of ten thousand dollars was confined to the operations of one year, and although the whole amount will not be required for such services during the current fiscal year, it will not, probably, be sufficient to cover the necessary expenditures of that character for two years.

JUDICIARY.

The expenditures from the judiciary fund, during the fiscal year ending June 30, 1861, were $727,000 61.   This includes the expenses of the courts, jurors, and witness' fees, rent and repairs of court-houses, and all other expenses attendant upon the administration of the laws of the federal judiciary, except the salaries of the judges, district attorneys, and marshals.

The suspension of the courts in several of the southern States will diminish the expenses of the judiciary to that extent; but what may be gained from this cause will be more than counterbalanced by extraordinary expenses in the northern States, occasioned by the insurrection, chargeable to the judiciary fund.

The annual rent of rooms occupied by the federal courts constitutes a large item of the expenses. As a matter of economy, as well as of convenience to all connected with the courts, it is desirable that the government should own the buildings required for that purpose.

The United States now own the buildings in which the courts are held at Portland and Bangor, in Maine; at Windsor and Rutland, in Vermont; at Boston, in Massachusetts; at Providence, in Rhode Island; at Buffalo, in New York; at Pittsburg, in Pennsylvania; at Wilmington, in Delaware; at Richmond, in Virginia; at Wilmington, in North Carolina; at Savannah, in Georgia; at Pensacola and St. Augustine, in Florida; at Mobile, in Alabama; at Pontotoc, in Mississippi; at St. Louis, in Missouri; at Chicago, in Illinois; at Cleveland and Cincinnati, in Ohio; at Indianapolis, in Indiana; at Detroit, in Michigan, and at Santa Fé, in New Mexico. Buildings to be so occupied are in process of erection by the government at Key West, in Florida; at Galveston, in Texas, and at Madison, in Wisconsin.

Much inconvenience is daily experienced for the want of a suitable court-house, owned by the government, in the city of New York. The building formerly known as Burton's Theatre has been occupied by the courts since 1858, at a rent of $16,000 per annum. The government has already expended over $30,000 in altering the building to adapt it to the wants of the courts, and in necessary repairs. To render it convenient and comfortable will require additional expenditures, which may be lost by the sale of the property. The lease contains a clause giving to the government the option of purchasing the property within three years, at the price of $215,000.

The time has elapsed, but it is understood that it may yet be purchased, within a reasonable time, for that price.

Mr. Burton has deceased since the date of the lease, and the settlement of his estate will probably require a sale of this property. If it should be sold to persons who would require the removal of the courts, the government would be subjected to great inconvenience and expense. In my judgment the best interests of the government require that the property should be purchased, and I recommend an appropriation for that purpose.

PUBLIC BUILDINGS.

The report of the Commissioner of Public Buildings exhibits the condition of the several interests confided to his charge.

The occupation of the Capitol during the past summer, by portions of the volunteer forces, necessarily caused some injury, which will require more than the ordinary appropriations for repairs.

The old portion of the building needs outside painting, as well to give uniformity of appearance to the whole, as to protect it from decay.

3 M

A portion of the basement of the building is now used as a bakery for the army. Although this may be submitted to for a time as a military necessity, it ought not to be permitted any longer than absolute necessity will require. Immediate provision should be made to transfer this useful branch of industry to some other locality, where it may be conducted without injury to the national Capitol, or annoyance to its occupants.

The subject of the extension of the Capitol grounds has heretofore occupied the attention of Congress. The private property necessary to make the proposed extension, has been appraised in conformity with the directions of an act of Congress, at the sum of $417,594 90.

The propriety of making a purchase involving so large an expenditure, at a time when the demands upon the Treasury for the support of the war, have rendered a resort to direct taxation necessary, must be determined by Congress. The Commissioner zealously advocates an early appropriation for that purpose, for, reasons which will be found upon reference to his report.

The improvements and repairs which have been made upon the several public buildings and other works during the past year, will be ascertained on reference to the Commissioner's report.

The Washington Infirmary, located upon Judiciary square, was destroyed by fire on the morning of the 3d instant. The fire is supposed to have originated from accidental causes, and when first discovered could have been readily extinguished by an efficient fire department.

Congress by an act approved June 15, 1844, directed the Commissioner of Public Buildings to allow the medical faculty of the Columbian College to occupy this building, (which had before been used as an insane hospital,) "for the purposes of an infirmary for medical instruction and for scientific purposes, on condition that they shall give satisfactory security to keep the said building in repair, and return it, with the grounds, to the government, in as good condition as they are now in, whenever required to do so." In 1853, Congress appropriated twenty thousand dollars "to aid the directors of Washington Infirmary to enlarge their accommodations for the benefit of sick transient paupers."

This sum was expended in enlarging and improving the building which has since been under the control of the medical faculty, under the authority conferred by the law of 1844.

During the last summer extensive hospital accommodations having become necessary from the large accumulation of troops on the Potomac an order was made by this department to place the building under the control of the War Department, to be used as an army hospital. It was accordingly occupied for that purpose up to the time of its destruction. I do not consider that any public necessity requires a reconstruction of the building.

Judiciary square, upon which it is situated, was designed for other purposes, and if the erection of an infirmary should be considered necessary, a different location should be sought. I recommend that provision be made for the removal of the walls of the building yet standing.

A street railroad through Pennsylvania avenue is a necessity which should no longer be disregarded. The great advantages of this mode of communication upon important city thoroughfares, have been so fully demonstrated in all the large cities of the United States, that no argument upon the subject will be required.

The repairs of Pennsylvania avenue have annually cost the government large sums, and the heavy transportation for army purposes which has passed over it this season will render necessary larger appropriations than those usually made.

It is probable that those who are asking from the government the privilege of constructing and using a railroad from the Navy Yard, through Pennsylvania avenue, to Georgetown, would, as a consideration for the privilege, agree to keep the avenue, at least between the Capitol and President's square, in good repair. If such an arrangement can be made, the government would avoid a large annual expense, while the citizens and those who visit the District would enjoy the great advantages of this most important improvement.

A new jail in the city of Washington is greatly needed.

The old jail is now crowded with more than double the number of persons of different colors and sexes than can be kept there with any regard to cleanliness or health. It is unfit for the purposes of a jail, and wholly inadequate to the demands made upon it. An appropriation for the erection of a new jail should be made by Congress.

PUBLIC PRINTING.

The change in the manner of executing the public printing, adopted by the last Congress, has been eminently successful. Under the direction of the present efficient superintendent the work has been performed with more despatch and at less cost to the government than at any previous time.

The system of executing the public printing in an office owned and controlled by the government was commenced on the 4th of March last. All the public printing and binding has not, since that time, been executed in the government office, for the reason that unexpired contracts have controlled a part of it.

The report of the Superintendent will show the cost to the government of the work already executed, and what would have been its cost under the prices established by the law of 1852.

It will be seen that there was a saving of $21,127 95 on so much of the printing of the 36th Congress as was done in his office, and $3,628 66 on that of the first session of the 37th Congress.

On the printing for the executive departments the saving amounts to 50 per cent.

Upon the binding for the executive departments there has been a saving of about $1,000 per month; but the binding for the 36th Congress having been done under a contract existing at the time the Government Printing Office was established, there has been no opportunity to show what might have been saved on that work.

The expenditures for paper, printing, binding, engraving, and lithographing have heretofore constituted a very large item in the expenses of the government. The orders of the 34th Congress for these objects involved an expenditure of $1,586,407 53. Of this amount $390,679 72 was paid for printing, $317,927 92 for engraving and lithographing, and $364,999 84 for binding. To this should be added the cost of the Daily and Congressional Globe for the same Congress, which was $257,904 28, and the printing for the executive departments for the same time, $152,883'04, making the whole expenditures for the two years $1,996,194 85. The cost of engraving and lithographing, from August, 1852, to December, 1858, was $892,139 59. This work can be done much more economically under the direction of the Superintendent of Public Printing than by the present contract system. The Superintendent can as well control and direct this part of the work as the printing, and without additional expense. At least fifty per cent of the present cost of engraving and lithographing can be saved by having it executed in the Government Printing Office.

HOSPITAL FOR THE INSANE.

The accompanying reports of the board of visitors and superintendent of the Government Hospital for the Insane, furnish full information of the progress and condition of this valuable and beneficient institution. Too much praise cannot be awarded to Dr. C. H. Nichols, the superintendent, for the ability and fidelity with which he has executed the important and delicate trusts confided to his charge.

The appropriations made by Congress for the erection of the buildings and the improvement of the grounds, have been expended with judgment and economy.

The buildings are spacious, well ventilated and warmed; admirably arranged with every convenience necessary for the health and comfort of patients, and in every respect are well adapted to the purposes for which they were designed. The grounds are in a fine state of improvement, and with but a small additional appropriation the whole may be completed and rendered an object of just pride to the country.

Since the institution was opened, in 1855, 439 persons have been treated. The number of patients in the house on the 30th June, 1861, was 180, classified as follows: From the army, 25; from the navy, 11; from the revenue cutter service, 1; from civil life, males 71 and females 72.

Of the inmates during the last fiscal year, 19 died, 63 were discharged, of whom 15 had so far improved that they could be safely removed, and 48 were completely recovered. The large proportion of patients who were discharged as recovered, (which was fifty per centum of the admissions,) furnishes ample evidence of the skill and care of the treatment observed.

The existing insurrection has thrown upon this institution largely increased burdens and responsibilities. During the first quarter of the current fiscal year, the admissions from the army and navy have been equal to four-fifths of the whole number of all classes admitted during the previous year. But in addition to the duties imposed upon him by law, Dr. Nichols has generously, with the approbation of this department, appropriated a portion of the building, with the services of himself and his assistant, for the accommodation of the sick and wounded of the Potomac and Chesapeake fleets.

As many as fifty persons of this class have been under treatment at one time. These extraordinary demands upon the resources of the institution will furnish ample reason for the request for slightly increased appropriations by Congress.

COLUMBIAN INSTITUTION FOR THE DEAF AND DUMB AND THE BLIND.

This institution was organized in 1857. The number of pupils at the close of the first year was but seventeen. At the close of the last fiscal year the number was thirty-five. The whole resources of the institution amount to but $8,126 19, of which $6,425 94 was appropriated by Congress. With such limited means but small results could be expected; but from the great liberality of the Hon. Amos Kendall, president of the board of directors, and his watchful care of the interests of the institution, much good has been accomplished.

The means of the institution have not been sufficient for the instruction of the pupils in horticulture, agriculture, and the mechanic arts. Instruction in these branches of industry is important, to prepare them to earn their own subsistence.

Additional appropriations to furnish the institution with the means to supply this deficiency in the instruction of the pupils are asked for by the board of directors, and are recommended to the favorable consideration of Congress.

The buildings now occupied do not afford the necessary space and accommodations for the number of pupils who now occupy them. An appropriation is asked for by the board of directors to make some additions which are greatly needed, and which I hope will be favorably considered.

The reports of the president of the board of directors and of the superintendent, are referred to for detailed information.

METROPOLITAN POLICE.

The metropolitan police, authorized by an act of Congress of August 6, 1861, has been organized in accordance with the provisions of the law.

The report of the board is herewith presented. They recommend several amendments to the law, and an increase of compensation, with an additional number of officers. The organization has been so recently effected that time has not been given to fairly test the sufficiency of the force employed, or the wisdom of the several provisions of the law. The views of the board are fully explained in their report, and the whole subject should be referred to Congress for such action as they may deem proper.

The number of convicts confined in the penitentiary on the 30th September, 1861, was 158, classified as follows: white males, 96; colored males, 54; white females, 2; colored females, 6.

One hundred and nine were natives of the United States, and forty-nine were of foreign birth.

Seventy-three convicts were received during the past year, and seventy-four discharged—sixty-one by the expiration of the term of sentence, thirteen by pardon of the President.

Ninety-six of the convicts are employed in the manufacture of shoes, and 25 in that of brooms. The others are employed in various branches of labor necessary to provide for the wants of the convicts and to keep the buildings in a proper condition of repair and cleanliness.

The expenses of the penitentiary during the fiscal year ending June 30, 1861, were $32,741 26. Of this sum $9,987 46 was received from sales of the products of the labor of the convicts; showing an excess of expenditures over receipts of $22,753 77.

It is evident that a considerable portion of this expense has been occasioned by improper management of the institution. This is shown by the great difference in the amount of the expenditures made by the present warden and those made by his predecessor during a corresponding period. The present warden entered upon his duties on the 12th April, 1861. From October 1, 1860, to that time— a period of six and a half months—there was expended for clothing, provisions, fuel and lights, and hospital stores, $13,118 50; for the same articles there was expended, from April 12 to October 1, 1861— a period of five and a half months—$4,566 70.

Under the administration of the present warden the labor of the convicts has been made productive. In the shoe manufactory, from April 12 to September 30, the receipts were $1,963 01 more than the cost of material and all other expenses, except the labor of the convicts. In the broom manufactory, for the same period, the receipts exceeded the expenditures $710 78.

The income from the labor of the convicts can, doubtless, under prudent management, be largely increased; but whether the institution can be made self-sustaining is a matter of much doubt.

The board of inspectors, who are gentlemen of ability and experience, think there are general causes for the inability of the institution to sustain itself, which are not likely to be obviated. Their report explains in detail their views.

The penitentiary buildings are very badly adapted to the purposes for which they were constructed. Circumscribed in extent, inconveniently arranged, and illy ventilated, they are much inferior to the prisons of most of the States. It can hardly be expected, however, that Congress, in the present condition of the country, will authorize the erection of new buildings; but while the old ones may be used for several years, and until the condition of the treasury will better justify the expenditure necessary to erect new ones, the health and comfort of the prisoners, and the convenience of all connected with the institution, require that an expenditure for improvements should be made, at least sufficient to introduce gas and the Potomac water. This can be done at a comparatively small cost, and an appropriation by Congress for that purpose is earnestly recommended.

I desire, in conclusion, to commend to your favorable notice the fidelity and zeal with which the various officers of the department have discharged the public trusts committed to them. Their several reports herewith show the extent of their labors, and exhibit a highly satisfactory condition of the business of the different branches of the department.

I have the honor to be, very respectfully, your obedient servant,

CALEB B. SMITH,
Secretary of the Interior.

To the PRESIDENT.

REPORT

OF

THE SECRETARY OF WAR

WAR DEPARTMENT, *December* 1, 1861.

SIR: I have the honor to submit the annual report of this Department.

The accompanying reports of the chiefs of the several Bureaus present the estimates of the appropriations required for the service of this Department during the fiscal year ending June 30, 1863, and also the appropriations necessary to cover deficiencies in the Estimates for 1861–'62:

The following statement presents the entire estimated strength of the army, both volunteers and regulars:

States.	Volunteers.		
	3 months.	For the war.	Aggregate.
California		4,688	4,688
Connecticut	2,236	12,400	14,636
Delaware	775	2,000	2,775
Illinois	4,941	80,000	84,941
Indiana	4,686	57,332	62,018
Iowa	968	19,800	20,768
Kentucky		15,000	15,000
Maine	768	14,239	15,007
Maryland		7,000	7,000
Massachusetts	3,435	26,760	30,195
Michigan	781	28,550	29,331
Minnesota		4,160	4,160
Missouri	9,356	22,130	31,486
New Hampshire	779	9,600	10,379
New Jersey	3,068	9,342	12,410
New York	10,188	100,200	110,388
Ohio	10,236	81,205	91,441
Pennsylvania	19,199	94,760	113,959
Rhode Island	1,285	5,898	7,183
Vermont	780	8,000	8,780
Virginia	779	12,000	12,779
Wisconsin	792	14,153	14,945
Kansas		5,000	5,000
Colorado		1,000	1,000
Nebraska		2,500	2,500
Nevada		1,000	1,000
New Mexico		1,000	1,000
District of Columbia	2,823	1,000	3,823
	77,875	640,637	718,512
Estimated strength of the regular army, including the new enlistments under act of Congress of July 29, 1861		20,334	
Total		660,971	

The several arms of the service are estimated as follows :

	Volunteers.	Regulars.	Aggregate.
Infantry	557,208	11,175	568,383
Cavalry	54,654	4,744	59,398
Artillery	20,380	4,308	24,688
Rifles and Sharpshooters	8,395		8,395
Engineers		107	107
	640,637	20,334	660,971

The appropriations asked for the service of the next fiscal year are computed for a force of 500,000 men. They have been reduced to the lowest possible amount consistent with the public interests, and are based upon a strictly economical administration of the various branches of this Department.

The appropriations to cover deficiencies are rendered necessary by the excess of the force in the field over that upon which the Estimates were founded, and by extraordinary expenditures connected with the employment and discharge of the Three Months' Contingent.

An item of very heavy expense is the large mounted force which has been organized, equipped, and made available since the called session of Congress, and which was not computed for in the Estimate. While an increase of Cavalry was undoubtedly necessary, it has reached a numerical strength more than adequate to the wants of the service. As it can only be maintained at a great cost, measures will be taken for its gradual reduction.

In organizing our great army, I was effectively aided by the loyal Governors of the different States, and I cheerfully acknowledge the prompt patriotism with which they responded to the call of this Department.

Congress, during its extra session, authorized the army to be increased by the acceptance of a volunteer force of 500,000 men, and made an appropriation of five hundred millions of dollars for its support. A call for the troops was immediately made ; but so numerous were the offers that it was found difficult to discriminate in the choice, where the patriotism of the people demanded that there should be no restriction upon enlistments. Every portion of the loyal States desired to swell the army, and every community was anxious that it should be represented in a cause that appealed to the noblest impulses of our people.

So thoroughly aroused was the national heart, that I have no doubt this force would have been swollen to a million, had not the Department felt compelled to restrict it, in the absence of authority from the representatives of the people to increase the limited number. It will be for Congress to decide whether the army shall be further augmented, with a view to a more speedy termination of the war, or whether it shall be confined to the strength already fixed by

law. In the latter case, with the object of reducing the volunteer
force to 500,000, I propose, with the consent of Congress, to consoli-
date such of the regiments as may from time to time fall below the
regulation standard. The adoption of this measure will decrease the
number of officers, and proportionably diminish the expenses of the
army.

It is said of Napoleon by Jomini that, in the campaign of 1815, that
great general on the 1st of April had a regular army of 200,000 men.
On the 1st of June he had increased this force to 414,000. The
like proportion, adds Jomini, "had he thought proper to inaugurate a
vast system of defence, would have raised it to 700,000 men by the
1st of September." At the commencement of this rebellion, inaugurated by the attack upon Fort Sumter, the entire military force at
the disposal of this Government was 16,006 Regulars, principally
employed in the West to hold in check marauding Indians. In April,
75,000 volunteers were called upon to enlist for three months' service, and responded with such alacrity that 77,875 were immediately
obtained. Under the authority of the act of Congress of July 22,
1861, the States were asked to furnish 500,000 volunteers to serve
for three years, or during the war; and by the act approved the 29th
of the same month, the addition of 25,000 men to the Regular Army
of the United States was authorized. The result is, that we have
now an army of upwards of 600,000 men. If we add to this the
number of the discharged Three months' Volunteers, the aggregate
force furnished to the Government since April last exceeds 700,000
men.

We have here an evidence of the wonderful strength of our institutions. Without conscriptions, levies, drafts, or other extraordinary
expedients, we have raised a greater force than that which, gathered
by Napoleon with the aid of all these appliances, was considered an
evidence of his wonderful genius and energy, and of the military spirit
of the French nation. Here every man has an interest in the Government, and rushes to its defence when dangers beset it.

By reference to the records of the Revolution it will be seen that
Massachusetts, with a population of 350,000, had at one time 56,000
troops in the field, or over one-sixth of her entire people—a force
greatly exceeding the whole number of troops furnished by all the
southern States during that war. Should the present loyal States
furnish troops in like proportion, which undoubtedly would be the case
should any emergency demand it, the Government could promptly
put into the field an army of over three millions.

It gives me great satisfaction to refer to the creditable degree of
discipline of our troops, most of whom were, but a short time since,
engaged in the pursuits of peace. They are rapidly attaining an
efficiency which cannot fail to bring success to our arms. Officers and
men alike evince an earnest desire to accomplish themselves in every
duty of the camp and field, and the various corps are animated by
an emulation to excel each other in soldierly qualities.

The conspiracy against the Government extended over an area of
733,144 square miles, possessing a coast line of 3,523 miles. and a

shore line of 25,414 miles, with an interior boundary line of 7,031 miles in length.   This conspiracy stripped us of arms and munitions, and scattered our navy to the most distant quarters of the globe. The effort to restore the Union, which the Government entered on in April last, was the most gigantic endeavor in the history of civil war. The interval of seven months has been spent in preparation.

The history of this rebellion, in common with all others, for obvious causes, records the first successes in favor of the insurgents. The disaster of Bull Run was but the natural consequence of the premature advance of our brave but undisciplined troops, which the impatience of the country demanded.   The betrayal also of our movements by traitors in our midst enabled the rebels to choose and intrench their position, and by a reinforcement in great strength, at the moment of victory, to snatch it from our grasp.   This reverse, however, gave no discouragement to our gallant people; they have crowded into our ranks, and although large numbers have been necessarily rejected, a mighty army in invincible array stands eager to precipitate itself upon the foe.   The check that we have received upon the Potomac has, therefore, but postponed the campaign for a few months.   The other successes of the rebels, though dearly won, were mere affairs, with no important or permanent advantages.   The possession of Western Virginia and the occupation of Hatteras and Beaufort have nobly redeemed our transient reverses.

At the date of my last report the States of Delaware, Maryland, Kentucky, and Missouri were threatened with rebellion.   In Delaware, the good sense and patriotism of the people have triumphed over the unholy schemes of traitors.   The people of Kentucky early pronounced themselves, by an unequivocal declaration at the ballot-box, in favor of the Union ; and Maryland, notwithstanding the efforts of bad men in power in the city of Baltimore, when the opportunity of a general election was afforded, under the lead of her brave and patriotic Governor, rebuked by an overwhelming majority the traitors who would have led her to destruction.   In Missouri a loyal State government has been established by the people, thousands of whom have rallied to the support of the Federal authority, and, in conjunction with troops from other portions of the country, have forced the rebels to retire into the adjoining State.   The government established in Virginia by the loyal portion of her population is in successful operation, and I have no doubt will be sustained by the people of the entire State whenever the thraldom of the rebel forces shall have been removed.

Thus has it been made clearly apparent that in whatever direction the forces of the Union have extended their protection, the repressed loyalty of the people, irresistibly manifesting itself, has aided to restore and maintain the authority of the Government; and I doubt not that the army now assembled on the banks of the Potomac, will, under its able leader, soon make such a demonstration as will reestablish its authority throughout all the rebellious States.

The loyal Governor of Virginia is proceeding to organize courts under the constitution and laws of the State in all her Eastern counties in the occupation of our troops. I respectfully suggest that authority should be given to the President to send commissioners with the army, with power to exercise all the functions of local government wherever the civil authority has ceased to exist, and especially to enforce the obligations of contracts, and the collection of debts due to loyal creditors.

As stated in my last Report, at the commencement of this rebellion the Government found itself deficient in arms and munitions of war, through the bad faith of those intrusted with their control during the preceding administration. The Armory at Harper's Ferry having been destroyed to prevent its possession and use by the rebels, the Government was compelled to rely upon the single armory at Springfield, and upon private establishments, for a supply of arms. Every effort has been made to increase the capacity of that armory, the greatest product of which, prior to these troubles, had never exceeded 800 muskets per month. In charge of an energetic and able Ordnance officer, the force being doubled, and operations vigorously prosecuted day and night, there were made at this establishment, during the past month of October, a total of 6,900 muskets; and it is confidently expected that 10,000 will be manufactured during the present month. On a recent visit, with a view to enlarge the capacity of the armory, I directed the purchase of a large quantity of machinery already finished, which, when put in operation, will enable this establishment to produce, during the next year, 200,000 stand of the justly celebrated Springfield rifles. I respectfully suggest the recommendation of a liberal appropriation by Congress for the purpose of yet further increasing the capacity of this Armory, believing that it can be made sufficient to supply all the muskets and rifles which the Government may hereafter need in any contingency. Located in a healthful country, in the midst of an industrious and ingenious people, where competent workmen can always be obtained without difficulty, and sufficiently near to all the materials needed in the manufacture of arms, it is at the same time accessible to every part of the country by water and railway communication.

After having made contracts for arms with the private establishments in this country, it was deemed necessary by the President, to insure a speedy and ample supply, to send a special agent to Europe with funds to the amount of two millions of dollars to purchase more. I am gratified to state that he has made arrangements for a large number of arms, part of which have already been delivered. The remainder will be shipped by successive steamers until all shall have been received.

Combinations among manufacturers, importers, and agents, for the sale of arms, have, in many cases, caused an undue increase in prices. To prevent advantage being thus taken of the necessities of the Government, Collectors of Customs have been directed to deliver to the agents of the United States all arms and munitions that may be imported into this country.

The demand for arms has called into existence numerous establishments for their manufacture throughout the loyal portion of the country, and it has been the policy of this Department to encourage the development of the capital, enterprise, and skill of our people in this direction. The Government should never have less than a million of muskets in its arsenals, with a corresponding proportion of arms and equipments for artillery and cavalry. Otherwise, it may, at a most critical moment, find itself deficient in guns while having an abundance of men.

I recommend that application be made to Congress for authority to establish a national foundry for the manufacture of heavy artillery at such point as may afford the greatest facilities for the purpose. While a sufficient number of cannon, perhaps, could be procured from private manufactories, the possession of a national establishment would lead to experiments which would be useful to the country, and prevent imposition in prices by the accurate knowledge that would be acquired of the real value of work of this character.

In my last report I called attention to the fact that legislation was necessary for the reorganization, upon a uniform basis, of the Militia of the country. Some general plan should be provided by Congress in aid of the States, by which our Militia can be organized, armed, and disciplined, and made effective at any moment for immediate service. If thoroughly trained in time of peace, when occasion demands, it may be converted into a vast army, confident in its discipline and unconquerable in its patriotism. In the absence of any general system of organization, upwards of 700,000 men have already been brought into the field; and, in view of the alacrity and enthusiasm that have been displayed, I do not hesitate to express the belief that no combination of events can arise in which this country will not be able not only to protect itself, but, contrary to its policy, which is peace with all the world, to enter upon aggressive operations against any power that may intermeddle with our domestic affairs. A committee should be appointed by Congress, with authority to sit during the recess, to devise and report a plan for the general organization of the Militia of the United States.

It is of great importance that immediate attention should be given to the condition of our Fortifications upon the seaboard and the Lakes, and upon our exposed frontiers. They should at once be placed in perfect condition for successful defence. Aggressions are seldom made upon a nation ever ready to defend its honor and to repel insults; and we should show to the world, that while engaged in quelling disturbances at home we are able to protect ourselves against attacks from abroad.

I earnestly recommend that immediate provision be made for increasing the corps of Cadets to the greatest capacity of the Military Academy. There are now only 192 cadets at that important institution. I am assured by the Superintendent that 400 can at present be accommodated, and that, with very trifling additional expense, this number may be increased to five hundred. It is not necessary, at this late day, to speak of the value of educated soldiers. While, in time of war or rebellion, we must ever depend mainly upon our Militia and Volunteers, we shall always need thoroughly trained officers. Two classes having been graduated during the present year, in order that the service might have the benefit of their military education, I had hoped that Congress, at its extra session, would authorize an increase of the number. Having failed to do so, I trust that at the approaching session an increase will be authorized, and that the selection of cadets will be limited exclusively to those States which, co-operating cordially with the Government, have brought their forces into the field to aid in the maintenance of its authority.

In this connexion, justice requires that I should call attention to the claims of a veteran officer, to whom, more than to any other, the Military Academy is indebted for its present prosperous and efficient condition. I allude to Colonel Sylvanus Thayer, of the Engineer corps, who now, by reason of advanced years and faithful public services, is incapacitated for duty in the field. Under the recent law of Congress he may justly claim to be retired from active service; but, believing that his distinguished services should receive some mark of acknowledgment from the government, I recommend that authority be asked to retire him upon his full pay and emoluments.

The health of an army is a consideration of the highest consequence. Good men and women in different States, impelled by the highest motives of benevolence and patriotism, have come in aid of the constituted sanitary arrangements of the government, and been greatly instrumental in diminishing disease in the camps, giving increased comfort and happiness to the life of the soldier, and imparting to our hospital service a more humane and generous character. Salubrity of situation and pleasantness of surroundings have dictated the choice of the hospital sites, and establishments for our sick and wounded, of which we have every reason to be proud, have been opened in St. Louis, Washington, Georgetown, Baltimore, and Annapolis, and will be attached to every division of the army in the field. To the close of the war vigilant care shall be given to the health of the well soldier, and to the comfort and recovery of the sick.

I recommend that the system of promotions which prevails in the Regular service be applied to the Volunteer forces in the respective States; restricting, however, the promotions to men actually in the field. At present each Governor selects and appoints the officers for the troops furnished by his State, and complaint is not unfrequently made, that when vacancies occur in the field, men of inferior qualifications are placed in command over those in the ranks who are their superiors in military experience and capacity. The advancement of merit should be the leading principle in all promotions, and the Volunteer soldier should be given to understand that preferment will be the sure reward of intelligence, fidelity, and distinguished service.

The course above recommended has been pursued by this Department, and it is my intention, so far as is in my power, to continue a system which cannot fail to have a most beneficial effect upon the entire service.

By existing laws and regulations an officer of the Regular army ranks an officer of Volunteers of the same grade, notwithstanding the commission of the latter may be of antecedent date. In my judgment, this practice has a tendency to repress the ardor and to limit the opportunity for distinction of Volunteer officers, and a change should be made by which seniority of commission should confer the right of command.

I submit for reflection the question, whether the distinction between Regulars and Volunteers which now exists, should be permitted to continue. The efficiency of the army, it appears to me, might be greatly increased by a consolidation of the two during the continuance of the war, which, combining both forces, would constitute them one grand army of the Union.

Recruiting for the Regular army has not been attended with that success which was anticipated, although a large number of men have entered this branch of the service. While it is admitted that soldiers in the Regular army, under the control of officers of military education and experience, are generally better cared for than those in the Volunteer service, it is certain that the popular preference is largely given to the latter. Young men evidently prefer to enter a corps officered by their friends and acquaintances, and, besides the bounty granted to volunteers in most of the States, inducements are often directly offered to them by those whose commissions depend upon their success in obtaining recruits. In addition, the Volunteer is allowed to draw his full pay of $13 per month, while by law $2 per month are deducted from the pay of the Regular, to be returned to him at the end of his term of service. In my judgment, this law should be repealed, and the Regular soldier be allowed to receive his full pay when due. He should also receive either a reasonable bounty upon enlisting, or an advance of $20 of the $100 which a law of the last session of Congress grants to regulars and volunteers on the expiration of their periods of service. This would doubtless stimulate enlistments, as it would enable the soldier to make some provision for those dependent upon him for support until he receives his pay.

By the Act approved August 5, 1861, the President is authorized to appoint as many aids to Major Generals of the Regular army, acting in the field, as he may deem proper. The number of aids, in my opinion, should be limited, and no more should be allowed to each Major General than can be advantageously employed upon his own proper staff. Much expense would thus be saved, and the Executive and this Department would be relieved of applications very embarrassing from their nature and extent.

The fifth section of the Act approved September 28, 1850, makes the discharge of minors obligatory upon this Department, upon proof that their enlistment was without the consent of their parents or guardians. In view of the injurious operation of this law, and of the facilities which it opens to frauds, I respectfully urge its early repeal. Applications for discharges of minors can then be determined either by this Department, in accordance with such regulations as experience may have shown to be necessary, or by the civil tribunals of the country.

The employment of Regimental Bands should be limited ; the proportion of musicians now allowed by law being too great, and their usefulness not at all commensurate with their heavy expense.

Corporations, like individuals, are liable to be governed by selfish motives in the absence of competition. An instance of this kind occurred in the management of the railroads between Baltimore and New York. The sum of $6 was charged upon that route for the transportation of each soldier from New York to Baltimore. As this rate seemed extravagant to the Department, when considered in connexion with the great increase of trade upon these roads, made necessary by the wants of the Government, inquiry was made concerning the expediency of using the roads from New York to Baltimore, *via* Harrisburg. The result was an arrangement by which troops were brought by the last-named route at $4 each; and, as a consequence, this rate was at once necessarily adopted by all the railroads in the loyal States, making a saving to the Government of 33⅓ per cent. in all its transportation of soldiers, and at the same time giving to the Railroads, through increased business, a liberal compensation.

The Railroad connexion between Washington and Baltimore has been lately much improved by additional sidings, and by extensions in this city. In order, however, that abundant supplies may always be at the command of the Department, arrangements should be made for laying a double track between this city and Annapolis Junction, with improved sidings and facilities at Annapolis and along the Branch road.

Should the navigation of the Potomac river be interrupted by blockade, or the severities of winter, it would become absolutely necessary, for the proper supply of the troops in the District of Columbia and vicinity, and of the inhabitants of this city, to provide additional railroad connexion between Washington and Baltimore. A responsible company, with a charter from the State of Maryland, have proposed to do this upon condition that the Government will indorse their bonds; they binding themselves to set aside annually a sufficient sum for their redemption at maturity, and thus eventually release the Government from any liability whatever, and to charge, for transportation, rates in no case to exceed four cents a ton per mile for freight, and three cents per mile for passengers. During the continuance of the war, however, their charge for passengers is not to exceed two cents per mile. The charge for the transportation of passengers between the two cities is at present 3¾ cents per mile, and for freight, the rates per ton will average from five to eight cents per mile. The large saving to the Government in cost of transportation, would amply compensate for all liability, and give to the citizens of all the loyal States greatly improved facilities for reaching the national capital, and at much less rates than they are now compelled to pay. To the citizens of the District it would cheapen the cost of supplies, and prove of immense value in every respect.

I recommend that a Railway be constructed through this city from the Navy Yard, by the Capitol, to Georgetown, forming connexions with the existing railroad depots, and using the Aqueduct bridge for the purpose of crossing the river at Georgetown. By a junction of this proposed railway with the Orange and Alexandria railroad, not only would the communication with our troops in Virginia be greatly improved, but an easy access be obtained to the Baltimore and Ohio railroad near Harper's Ferry, by means of the Loudon and Hampshire railroad. To its importance as affording facilities for moving troops and supplies in time of war, may be added the future benefits it would confer upon the District of Columbia. The outlay required would be saved in a few months by enabling the Government to dispense with the expensive ferry at Georgetown, and by greatly decreasing the costly wagon transportation of the army through this city.

The injuries to railroads, instigated by the rebel authorities of Baltimore, in order to embarrass communication with the North and West, *via* Harrisburg, and with the East, *via* Philadelphia, have been repaired by the different companies that own them. That portion of the Baltimore and Ohio railroad West of Harper's Ferry which was so ruthlessly destroyed by the rebels, has not yet been restored. The great interests of trade require that this road should be re-opened as speedily as possible by the company, for the transportation of the immense surplus of the agricultural productions of the West. To aid this object the Department has tendered to the company a sufficient force for its protection during the progress of the work, and will render such facilities as it may be able to provide, in connexion with its other important public duties.

For the purpose of facilitating the transportation of supplies to Alexandria and to points beyond, it has been found necessary to rebuild portions of the Orange and Alexandria and the Loudon and Hampshire railroads, and to lay a track from the Railroad depot to a point on the Potomac river, in this city.

Under an appropriation granted for that purpose at the last session of Congress, a Telegraphic Bureau was established, and has been found of the greatest service in our military operations. Eight hundred and fifty-seven miles of telegraphic line have been already built and put in operation, with an efficient corps of operators, and a large extension is now in process of construction.

Congress, at its late session, made an appropriation for the reconstruction of the Long Bridge across the Potomac, which, in its then dilapidated condition, was unsafe for military purposes. The work, which has been carried on without interruption to trade or travel, is rapidly approaching completion, and, when finished, will be a substantial structure.

On the first of the present month Lieutenant General Winfield Scott voluntarily relinquished his high command as General-in-chief of the American army. He had faithfully and gallantly served his country for upwards of half a century, and the glory of his achievements has given additional lustre to the brightest pages of our national annals. The affections of a grateful people followed him into his retirement. The President immediately conferred the command of the army upon the officer next in rank. Fortunately for the country, Major General McClellan had proved himself equal to every situation in which his great talents had been called into exercise. His brilliant achievements in Western Virginia, the untiring energy and consummate ability he has displayed in the organization and discipline of an entirely new army, have justly won for him the confidence and applause of the troops and of the nation.

Extraordinary labor, energy, and talent have been required of the various Bureaus of this Department to provide for the wants of our immense army. While errors may have been occasionally committed by subordinates, and while extravagant prices have undoubtedly in some cases, controlled by haste and the pressure of rapid events, been paid for supplies, it is with great gratification that I refer to the economical administration of affairs displayed in the various branches of the service. Our forces had not only to be armed, clothed, and fed, but had to be suddenly provided with means of transportation to an extent heretofore unparalelled. While I believe that there is no army in the world better provided for in every respect than our Regulars and Volunteers, I candidly think that no force so large, and so well equipped, was ever put in the field in so short a space of time at so small an expense.

While it is my intention to preserve the strictest economy and accountability, I think the last dollar should be expended and the last man should be armed to bring this unholy rebellion to a speedy and permanent close.

The geographical position of the metropolis of the nation, menaced by the rebels, and required to be defended by thousands of our troops, induces me to suggest for consideration the propriety and expediency of a reconstruction of the boundaries of the States of Delaware, Maryland, and Virginia. Wisdom and true statesmanship would dictate that the seat of the National Government, for all time to come, should be placed beyond reasonable danger of seizure by enemies within, as well as from capture by foes from without. By agreement between the States named, such as was effected, for similar purposes, by Michigan and Ohio, and by Missouri and Iowa, their boundaries could be so changed as to render the Capital more remote than at present from the influence of State governments which have arrayed themselves in rebellion against the Federal authority. To this end, the limits of Virginia might be so altered as to make her boundaries consist of the Blue Ridge on the East and Pennsylvania on the North, leaving those on the South and West as at present. By this arrangement, two counties of Maryland (Alleghany and Washington) would be transferred to the jurisdiction of Virginia. All that portion of Virginia which lies between the Blue Ridge and Chesapeake bay could then be added to Maryland, while that portion of the peninsula between the waters of the Chesapeake and the Atlantic, now jointly held by Maryland and Virginia, could be incorporated into the State of Delaware. A reference to the map will show that these are great natural boundaries, which, for all time to come, would serve to mark the limits of these States.

To make the protection of the Capital complete, in consideration of the large accession of territory which Maryland would receive under the arrangement proposed, it would be necessary that that State should consent so to modify her constitution as to limit the basis of her representation to her white population.

In this connexion, it would be the part of wisdom to reannex to the District of Columbia that portion of its original limits which by act of Congress was retroceded to the State of Virginia.

It is already a grave question what shall be done with those slaves who were abandoned by their owners on the advance of our troops into southern territory, as at Beaufort district, in South Carolina. The number left within our control at that point is very considerable, and similar cases will probably occur. What shall be done with them? Can we afford to send them forward to their masters, to be by them armed against us, or used in producing supplies to sustain the rebellion? Their labor may be useful to us; withheld from the enemy it lessens his military resources, and withholding them has no tendency to induce the horrors of insurrection, even in the rebel communities. They constitute a military resource, and, being such, that they should not be turned over to the enemy is too plain to discuss. Why deprive him of supplies by a blockade, and voluntarily give him men to produce them?

The disposition to be made of the slaves of rebels, after the close of the war, can be safely left to the wisdom and patriotism of Congress. The Representatives of the People will unquestionably secure to the loyal slaveholders every right to which they are entitled under the Constitution of the country.

SIMON CAMERON,
Secretary of War.

To the PRESIDENT.

REPORT

OF

THE SECRETARY OF THE NAVY.

NAVY DEPARTMENT, *December* 2, 1861.

SIR: The Report from this department under date of 4th July last exhibited the condition of the navy, the administrative measures taken to augment its efficiency, and the general course of its operations up to the commencement of the late special session of Congress. The enlarged estimates of expenditure for the naval service then submitted, contemplated, especially, three different lines of naval operations, upon an extended scale, as demanded by the situation of the country. These were—

1. The closing of all the insurgent ports along a coast line of nearly three thousand miles, in the form and under the exacting regulations of an international blockade, including the naval occupation and defence of the Potomac river, from its mouth to the federal capital, as the boundary line between Maryland and Virginia, and also the main commercial avenue to the principal base of our military operations.

2. The organization of combined naval and military expeditions to operate in force against various points of the southern coast, rendering efficient naval co-operation with the position and movements of such expeditions when landed, and including also all needful naval aid to the army in cutting off intercommunication with the rebels and in its operations on the Mississippi and its tributaries; and,

3. The active pursuit of the piratical cruisers which might escape the vigilance of the blockading force and put to sea from the rebel ports.

These were duties which the navy was called upon at the same time to prepare for and perform, and they constituted a triple task more arduous, it is believed, in some respects, than has before been demanded from the maritime power of any government. I proceed to report briefly the efforts which have been made for its accomplishment.

The limited number of ships and men at command when the proclamation announcing the blockade of the ports of the insurgent States was issued, and the inadequate means provided by the last Congress for the emergency, devolved upon the department the necessity for calling into immediate service not only all the naval forces but vessels from the commercial marine. Purchases were accordingly made and charters hastily executed for the exigency, and orders peremptorily issued to forthwith equip and prepare for service the public vessels that were dismantled and in ordinary at the several yards. The force thus hastily gathered was placed along our coast and divided into two squadrons, one of which, designated as the Atlantic blockading squadron, had for its field of operation the whole coast, extending from the easternmost line of Virginia to Cape Florida, and was under the command of Flag Officer Silas H. Stringham. The other, or Gulf squadron, operating from Cape Florida westward to the Rio Grande, was commanded by Flag Officer William Mervine. These officers repaired to their stations and were reinforced from time to time by the arrival of such vessels as were despatched to their commands, and under their supervision and direction all the ports upon their stations were subjected to a blockade as rigid and effective as the peculiar nature of our maritime frontier, which has through a large portion of its entire extent a double coast, inner and outer, would admit. Our principal naval vessels are not, from their great draft of water, adapted to blockade service on our shallow coast, which has been guarded with extreme difficulty. The ports of North Carolina especially, situated within the interior shallow waters of their sounds and inlets, afforded peculiar facilities to a class of small vessels, aided by fraudulent papers and foreign flags, to elude the vigilance of the sentinel ships whose special duty it was to interdict commerce with the insurgents.

THE POTOMAC FLOTILLA.

It became necessary at an early period to place a flotilla on the lower Potomac. A variety of circumstances combined to render this one of the most embarrassing duties on the whole insurgent frontier, and it was early foreseen by the department that without the active co-operation of the army it would be impossible to prevent the navigation of the river from being obstructed by batteries on the Virginia side. For several months, however, the navy, without aid, succeeded, more effectually than could have been expected, in keeping the river open for commercial purposes, and restricting, to a great extent, communication between the opposite shores. In the heroic discharge of this duty the first commander of the flotilla lost his life; but the navy continued to capture every rebel vessel which showed itself on the Potomac, and to give security and protection to the commerce of loyal citizens, until the close of October, when the insurgents erected batteries at sundry points on the Virginia shore, thereby rendering passage on the river dangerous.

THE SQUADRONS.

The duty of guarding the coast and enforcing the blockade has been one of great labor as well as ceaseless vigilance and responsibility. With the steadily increasing force that added to the squadrons, the efforts of the insurgents to elude our ships were also increased, in order to supply the pressing necessities that afflicted the whole of the rebel States. The duties imposed upon the flag officers became correspondingly arduous, and eventually more extensive in their operation and detail than could be well executed by one commander. While the subject of a division of the squadrons was under consideration, Flag Officer Stringham, unaware of the fact, made a proposition to relinquish his command, which was acceded to, and two squadrons were organized on the Atlantic coast. Capt. Louis M. Goldsborough was appointed to guard the shores of Virginia and North Carolina, and raised his flag on the Minnesota on the 23d of September. The residue of the southern Atlantic coast, commencing at the line which separates the two Carolinas and extending to Cape Florida, was intrusted to Capt. Samuel F. Dupont, whose flag was raised on the Wabash, on the 29th of October.

Flag Officer William Mervine was relieved from the command of the Gulf squadron in September by Capt. William W. McKean. The necessity of dividing this squadron, as well as that on the Atlantic seaboard, in order that the coast should be more rigidly guarded, was felt; but the measure was postponed until a larger force could be sent around the peninsula. A vigilant watch has been maintained at the passes of the Mississippi, by which the commerce of New Orleans has been successfully interdicted.

The task of blockading the coast is unattractive and devoid of adventure. Those who have engaged in this rebellion have neither commerce nor a navy to reward or stimulate to exertion.

SINKING VESSELS.

One method of blockading the ports of the insurgent States, and interdicting communication as well as to prevent the egress of privateers which sought to depredate on our commerce, has been that of sinking in the channels vessels laden with stone. The first movement in this direction was on the North Carolina coast, where there are numerous inlets to Albemarle and Pamlico sounds, and other interior waters, which afforded facilities for eluding the blockade, and also to the privateers. For this purpose a class of small vessels were purchased in Baltimore, some of which have been placed in Ocracoke inlet.

Another and larger description of vessels were bought in the eastern market, most of them such as were formerly employed in the whale fisheries. These were sent to obstruct the channels of Charleston harbor and the Savannah river ; and this, if effectually done, will prove the most economical and satisfactory method of interdicting commerce at those points.

VESSELS CAPTURED.

Since the institution of the blockade one hundred and fifty-three vessels have been captured sailing under various flags, most of which were attempting to violate the blockade. With few exceptions, these vessels were in such condition, when seized, as to authorize their being sent at once to the courts for adjudication and condemnation as prizes. Appended to this report is a list of the vessels which have been captured.

SEIZURE OF SOUTHERN PORTS.

A seizure of some of the important ports on the coast commanded the early and earnest attention of this department. It was found that naval stations and harbors of refuge during the tempestuous seasons would be indispensable if hostilities were to be continued, and the stations thus secured could also be made the points of offensive military operations. Shortly after the attention of the government was drawn to this subject, a board was convened under the auspices of the Navy Department, consisting of Captains Samuel F. Dupont and Charles H. Davis, of the navy; Major John G. Barnard, of the army, and Professor Alexander Bache, of the coast survey, to whom a thorough investigation of the coast and harbors, their access and defences, was committed. Several elaborate and valuable reports of great interest, exhibiting in minute detail the position, advantages, and topographical peculiarities of almost every eligible point on the coast, were the results of this important commission.

In view of the data thus presented, two combined naval and military expeditions have already been organized and put in action. Such co-operation and concert of action between the two arms of the public service were indispensable; for, though the navy alone might assail and capture batteries in some positions, it was not within its province or power to retain or garrison them. The operations on shore manifestly pertained to the army, and, on each occasion, as soon as the military forces were ready for these expeditions, the navy was fully prepared and eager for immediate action.

After some delays, an expedition to Hatteras inlet, on the coast of North Carolina, where piratical depredations had become extremely annoying, was undertaken. Flag Officer Stringham commanded in person the naval forces on this occasion, and Major General Butler had command of the small military detachment of about eight hundred men which co-operated with the navy. The expedition was eminently successful in the attack upon and capture of Forts Hatteras and Clark. The entire garrison, under the command of Samuel

Barron, recently and for nearly fifty years an officer of the navy, surrendered after sustaining great loss, while not a life was sacrificed nor an individual of the Union forces wounded. Annexed is the report of Flag Officer Stringham of this achievement, with the letter of approval and congratulation of this department. The military force was inadequate to follow up this brilliant victory by securing a position upon the main land, and there propitiating and protecting the loyal feeling which had begun to develop itself in North Carolina.

It was intended that the success at Hatteras should have been followed in September by a more formidable expedition, and the seizure of a more important position further south. Owing to various causes, independent of the Navy Department or the condition of the navy, this movement was unavoidably postponed until the 29th of October, when a fleet of forty-eight sail, including transports, a larger squadron than ever before assembled under our flag, left Hampton Roads. Capt. Samuel F. Dupont, then recently appointed flag officer, an officer of great skill and experience, and possessing the entire confidence of the department, was selected to command this expedition. In addition to his general professional ability, he had, through careful study and investigation, as chairman of the board which had been ordered in June, special qualification and thorough preparation for the highly important and responsible position assigned to him. Informed of the policy and views of the government in regard to the expedition, prompt to execute its wishes, and having made himself familiar with every eligible port on the southern Atlantic coast, he, as commander of the expedition, was intrusted with the selection, within prescribed limits, of the place where the first assault should be made.

After encountering the severest storm that has visited the coast during the present season, which partially dispersed the squadron, causing the wreck of several of the transports, and compelling even some of the smaller vessels of the navy to put back, the fleet, by the merciful interposition of Providence, was preserved, and appeared before Port Royal, one of the best, though neglected, harbors on our southern coast, on the 5th day of November. So soon as the channel could be buoyed out, and other preliminary measures accomplished, assaults were made on the well built and thoroughly armed forts, Beauregard and Walker. Consummate naval strategic skill and the most admirable gunnery were exhibited in the attack, which was of such tremendous effect that General Drayton and the rebel army surrendered their strongholds, fled the coast with precipitation, leaving their property, armament, and papers, while our naval forces took, and still hold, quiet possession of one of the finest harbors on the Atlantic seaboard. I append Flag Officer Dupont's report of this brilliant achievement, and the letter of this department congratulating him, his officers and men, on their bravery, skill, and success.

A demonstration since ordered by Flag Officer Dupont on Tybee island, at the mouth of the Savannah river, resulted in the capture of that island and the strong Martello tower and battery that virtually command Fort Pulaski. Our naval forces have possession of that island, a part of the south Atlantic squadron is at anchor in the harbor, and the flag of the Union is again unfurled in Georgia. The despatch of Flag Officer Dupont, communicating to the Navy Department an account of this transaction, and the additional fact that the rebels themselves have, in anticipation of our action, placed obstructions in the river at Fort Pulaski, is appended to the report.

Without specifying, in detail, the numerous meritorious achievements which have during the year done honor to the naval service, I append despatches of the commanders, communicating the brave and heroic conduct which has been displayed by our naval officers, sailors, and marines, whose intrepidity, courage, and loyalty were never more marked than in this rebellion.

THE MISSISSIPPI RIVER.

A naval force, auxilliary to and connected with the army movements on the Mississippi and its tributaries, has been organized, and is under the command of Flag Officer Andrew H. Foote, who is rendering efficient service in that quarter.

The steamers which have been built or purchased for this service by the War Department are of a formidable character, and manned by a class of superior seamen and western boatmen, who, in the preliminary skirmishes already, have done good service, and will, I am confident, acquit themselves with credit in the future. Reports are appended exhibiting some of the operations of this command as auxiliary to the military movements on the Mississippi.

PURSUIT OF PRIVATEERS.

It was natural that apprehensions should prevail in regard to armed cruisers commissioned expressly by the rebel leaders to depredate upon our commerce. This robbery of merchants and others engaged in peaceful and lawful pursuits by piratical cruisers is not inconsistent with the general conduct of those who have violated law and moral obligations to gratify inordinate ambition. Our extended commerce presented inducements for piratical warfare, yet but few of our misguided countrymen have prostituted themselves to the purposes of plunder, though thereto invited, and these few have been in constant flight to escape the avenging power of our vigilant naval forces. Such of these cruisers as eluded the blockade and capture were soon wrecked, beached, or sunk, with the exception of one, the steamer Sumter, which, by some fatality, was permitted to pass the Brooklyn, then blockading one of the passes of the Mississippi, and, after a brief and feeble chase by the latter, was allowed to proceed on her piratical voyage. An investigation of this whole occurrence was ordered by the department. Soon the Niagara and the Powhatan, from the Gulf squadron, followed in vigorous pursuit—the latter, though long in commission, and with defective boilers and machinery, under her energetic commander, tracking the piratical craft as far as Maranham. The Keystone State, Richmond, Iroquois, and San Jacinto were also in search of her at different points and periods. Although a piratical rover, without license from any recognized or acknowledged government, and avowedly engaged in the robbery and plunder of our citizens, I regret to say this vessel has been received, and her wants supplied, against the remonstrance of our consuls, by public authorities, in many foreign ports where her character was well known.

REBEL EMISSARIES.

Capt. Charles Wilkes, in command of the San Jacinto, while searching in the West Indies for the Sumter, received information that James M. Mason and John Slidell, disloyal citizens and leading conspirators, were with their suite to embark from Havana in the English steamer "Trent," on their way to Europe to promote the cause of the insurgents. Cruising in the Bahama channel he intercepted the Trent on the 8th of November, and took from her these dangerous men, whom he brought to the United States. His vessel having been ordered to refit for service at Charleston, the prisoners were retained on board and conveyed to Fort Warren, where they were committed to the custody of Colonel Dimmick, in command of that fortress.

The prompt and decisive action of Captain Wilkes on this occasion merited and received the emphatic approval of the department, and if a too generous forbearance was exhibited by him in not capturing the vessel which had these rebel enemies on board, it may, in view of the special circumstances, and of its patriotic motives, be excused; but it must by no means be permitted to constitute a precedent hereafter for the treatment of any case of similar infraction of neutral obligations by foreign vessels engaged in commerce or the carrying trade.

THE NAVAL FORCE AND ITS INCREASE.

This brief review of the principal operations of the navy, under the new and extraordinary demands that were made upon its efficiency, naturally introduces an exposition of the measures adopted in conformity with the legislative policy of Congress to increase its available force. The measures which were adopted by the department, in advance of the special session in July, for augmenting the navy, and the recommendations and suggestions which I had the honor at that time to submit, received the sanction and approval of Congress. Immediate action had been rendered necessary in consequence of events that had been precipitated upon the country, and for which no legislative provision had been made. Only a feeble force of men and vessels, scarcely sufficient for ordinary police operations, was at that time available on the Atlantic coast. In order that the condition of the navy on the 4th of March may be rightly understood, it will be well to state the position and character of each of the vessels at that date.

The home squadron consisted of twelve vessels, and of these only four were in northern ports and available for service, viz:

Name.	Class.	No. of guns.	Where stationed.
Pawnee	Screw sloop	8	At Washington.
Crusader	Steamer	8	At New York.
Mohawk	Steamer	5	do.
Supply	Storeship	4	do.
4 vessels		25	

The remaining vessels of the squadron were stationed as follows:

Name.	Class.	No. of guns.	Where stationed.
Sabine	Frigate	50	Pensacola.
St. Louis	Sloop	20	do.
Brooklyn	Steamer	25	do.
Wyandotte	Steamer	5	do.
Macedonian	Sloop	22	Vera Cruz.
Cumberland	Sloop	24	} Returning from Vera Cruz.
Pocahontas	Steamer	5	
Powhatan	Steamer	11	
8 vessels		162	

The Powhatan arrived at New York on the 12th of March, and sailed early in April for Fort Pickens. The Pocahontas reached Hampton Roads on the 12th of March, and the Cumberland on the 23d of the same month.

Of vessels on foreign stations, the following have returned in obedience to orders from the department:

FROM MEDITERRANEAN.

Name.	Class.	No. of guns.	Date of arrival.
Richmond	Steam sloop	16	July 3.
Susquehanna	Steam sloop	15	June 6.
Iroquois	Steam sloop	6	June 15.

FROM COAST OF AFRICA.

Name.	Class.	No. of guns.	Date of arrival.
Constellation	Sloop	22	September 28.
Portsmouth	Sloop	22	September 23.
Mohican	Steam sloop	6	September 27.
Mystic	Steamer	5	October 7.
Sumter	Steamer	5	September 15.
San Jacinto	Steam sloop	13	November 15.
Relief	Storeship	2	October 12.

FROM COAST OF BRAZIL.

Name.	Class.	No. of guns.	Date of arrival.
Congress	Frigate	50	August 12.
Seminole	Steam sloop	5	July 6.

The following have not yet arrived.

FROM EAST INDIES.

Name.	Class.	No. of guns.	Date of arrival.
John Adams	Sloop	20	
Hartford	Steam sloop	16	
Dacotah	Steam sloop	6	

The following are to remain abroad :

Name.	Class.	No. of guns.	Where stationed.
Saratoga	Sloop	18	Coast of Africa.
Pulaski	Steamer	1	Coast of Brazil.
Saginaw	Steamer	3	East Indies.

Add to these the vessels on the Pacific coast, the steam frigate Niagara, which was returning from Japan, and four tenders and storeships, and there was a total, as stated in the last report, of 42 vessels, carrying 555 guns and about 7,600 men, in commission on the 4th of March last.

Without waiting the arrival of vessels from our foreign squadrons, the department early directed such as were dismantled and in ordinary at the different navy yards, and which could be made available, to be repaired and put in commission. They are, exclusive of those lost at the Norfolk navy yard, embraced in the following table:

Names.	Where.	Ordered to be prepared for sea service with despatch.		Put in commission or ready for officers and crew.		Sailed.	
Frigates.		1861.		1861.		1861.	
Potomac	New York	April	27	July	30	Sept.	10
St. Lawrence	Philadelphia	April	20	Late in May		June	29
Santee	Portsmouth, N.H.	April	17	May	27	June	20
Sloops.							
Savannah	New York	April	1	June	1	July	10
Jamestown	Philadelphia	April	9	May	18	June	8
Vincennes	Boston	...do		June	24	July	12
Marion	Portsmouth	April	20	June	30	July	14
Dale	...do	...do		...do		July	17
Preble	Boston	...do		June	22	July	11
Brigs.							
Bainbridge	Boston	April	20	May	1	May	21
Perry	New York	...do				May	14
Steamers.							
Roanoke	New York	April	20	June	20	June	25
Colorado	Boston	...do		June	3	June	18
Minnesota	...do	April	3	May	2	May	8
Wabash	New York	April	9	April	29	May	30
Pensacola	Washington						
Mississippi	Boston	April	6	May	18	May	23
Water Witch	Philadelphia	Feb.	14	April	10	April	17

When the vessels now building and purchased, of every class, are armed, equipped, and ready for service, the condition of the navy will be as follows:

OLD NAVY.

Number of vessels.	Guns.	Tonnage.
6 Ships-of-Line	504	16,094
7 Frigates	350	12,104
17 Sloops	342	16,031
2 Brigs	12	539
3 Store-ships	7	342
6 Receiving ships, &c.	106	6,340
6 Screw frigates	222	21,460
6 First class screw-sloops	109	11,953
4 First class side-wheel steam sloops	46	8,003
8 Second class screw-sloops	45	7,593
5 Third class screw-sloops	28	2,405
4 Third class side-wheel steamers	8	1,808
2 Steam tenders	4	599
76	1,783	105,271

PURCHASED VESSELS.

•	Guns.	Tons.
36 side-wheel steamers	160	26,680
43 screw steamers	175	20,403
13 ships	52	9,998
24 schooners	49	5,324
18 barks	78	8,432
2 brigs	4	460
136	518	71,297

VESSELS CONSTRUCTED.

	Guns.	Tons.
14 screw sloops	98	16,787
23 gun-boats	92	11,661
12 side-wheel steamers	48	8,400
3 iron-clad steamers	18	4,600
52	256	41,448

Making a total of 264 vessels, 2,557 guns, and 218,016 tons. The aggregate number of seamen in the service on the 4th of March last was 7,600. The number is now not less than 22,000.

CONSTRUCTION OF NEW VESSELS.

Most of the public armed vessels being of such size and draught of water that they could render only imperfect blockading service, immediate measures were taken by the department to carry into effect the policy of the government, in advance of the special session of Congress, by contracting for the construction of twenty-three steamers, which should be of light draught, but heavy armament. Congress, at the regular session, had authorized the building of seven screw steamers, and as there were four yards, in each of which two might be built, the department, in the existing emergency, and in anticipation of the action of Congress when it should convene, directed the construction of eight, dividing them into two classes of about one thousand and fourteen hundred tons, respectively. At the special session, Congress not only sanctioned the action of the department in the construction of these thirty-one steamers, but it authorized the further construction of twelve side-wheel steamers of light draught, and of six of larger capacity, to be modelled and built specially for speed. Many of those first ordered are already in commission, and the others are in rapid progress towards completion. If, with those above enumerated, we include three iron-clad, or armor steamers, which are being built from the money appropriated for that purpose at the special session, there will be under these several arrangements an addition, when they are completed, of fifty-two new steamers. peculiarly adapted to the required blockade or coast guard duty, added to the navy. No sailing vessels have been ordered to be built, for steam, as well as heavy ordnance, has become an indispensable element of the most efficient naval power.

PURCHASE OF VESSELS.

The public vessels and the public yards, in their capacity of construction and repair, were, however, totally inadequate to the demands that are now pressing on this branch of the government, and the department was compelled to resort to the commercial marine to make good the deficiency. Vessels of every class and description were promptly tendered by sellers and their agents, who, in many instances, became dissatisfied when their offers were not accepted.

This new necessity of the government, involving a large expenditure, and the purchase of suitable vessels, imposed an important responsibilty; and the task of making suitable arrangements to insure the prompt and systematic purchase, on the best and most reasonable terms for the government, of a large number of vessels most suitable for its use, was attended by peculiar difficulties, and received mature consideration. The purchase might be made directly by the department, or by boards of officers under its control at the principal ports where the vessels were to be bought, and especially at the great central point of supply for such a demand, the port of New York.

But to both these methods of procedure the briefest trial disclosed serious objections. It was manifest from the first that the department, charged suddenly with the organization and superintendence of new and arduous naval operations on a large scale, in addition to its current business, could not possibly itself devote to the numerous details of each case of purchase the time and attention needful fully to protect the interests of the government. It was equally clear that boards of officers, acting in a mere mercantile capacity, new to them, and for which they had neither been practically trained nor professionally commissioned, would be subjected to great embarrassment and disadvantage in their dealings with sellers of ships and professional ship brokers, in a market suddenly pressed by a heavy and peremptory demand. Yet the department could rely, and it did rely, with the fullest confidence upon the professional judgment and ability of its ordnance officers, naval constructors, and engineers, all acting under the responsibility of their commissions, to investigate and determine the whole question of the adaptation, in all respects, of each ship offered, and of its capacity to be by alteration fully adapted to perform the particular service required by the government. This work, with the corresponding authority of selection and rejection of all vessels, was therefore exclusively committed to boards consisting each of an experienced naval constructor and engineer and an ordnance officer, convened and stationed for the purpose at New York, and the other principal cities. The mere mercantile part of the business—the making of the best bargains possible for the government in each case, with the care of averting all intervention of third parties, which might embarrass the attainment of that result—was considered by the government to be placed most properly in the hands of a mercantile agency of a high and established character for integrity, experience, and capacity. Obvious reasons, including the consideration that it is individual responsibility which is always felt most keenly, and that several agents, all acting separately for the government at the same places, would necessarily compete with each other to its disadvantage in the market, indicated that this agency should be tendered to a single, properly qualified individual, upon the distinct understanding that he should devote his whole time, attention, and ability to the work; that he should in no case make any charge against the government for his service; that he should deal always directly and exclusively with the owners of the vessels purchased, thus permitting no brokerage fees, or agents' commissions, between himself and the owners; and that, finally, his own commission, payable always by the seller, should in no case exceed the regular mercantile percentage fixed by the Chamber of Commerce of New York, and established by the custom of merchants in that city as the rightful and legal rate of remuneration for such services rendered by any person acting between the sellers and purchasers of vessels.

The agent thus selected was a merchant, who had been connected with one of the most successful and extensive commercial firms in this country—a gentleman of great business capacity, and of the most scrupulous and unquestioned integrity. Relinquishing all private engagements, and withdrawing from all business connexions of every

5 M

description, this gentleman has devoted his whole time and energies with untiring fidelity to the service of the department and the country.

By the system thus adopted the very best vessels in the commercial marine have been secured for the naval service at moderate rates, and to the great advantage of the government. The course pursued in these purchases has extemporized a navy at less cost to the government, it is believed, than that required for the construction of the same or equally serviceable vessels ; and a question which, at the commencement, was. one of embarrassment and difficulty, has been disposed of, and in no particular has the country been better served.

Subjoined is a statement from the purchasing agent at New York, with a schedule giving the name, tonnage, price demanded, and cost actually paid of every vessel that has been bought by him, and also of all added to the navy since the change of administration in March last. There is abundant reason to congratulate ourselves that, on such a demand, in such a crisis, we were enabled to make so speedy and so large an acquisition to the naval service, and on terms so economical to the government.

The expenditure in fitting for sea service the vessels at the different navy yards, and repairing and equipping those returning from our foreign squadrons, has been large. Eleven thousand mechanics and laborers have been in the daily employ of the government at the different navy yards in building and preparing vessels, and equipping and arming them for service ; but this large force has been unable to despatch the work with the rapidity demanded, and the department has been compelled in consequence to resort to private shipyards and outside labor.

ARMORED SHIPS.

To carry into effect the provisions of the act approved August 3, 1861, providing for the construction of one or more armored ships and floating batteries, I appointed Commodores Joseph Smith and Hiram Paulding and Captain Charles H. Davis, skilful and experienced naval officers, to investigate the plans and specifications that might be submitted. The subject of iron armature for ships is one of great general interest, not only to the navy and country, but is engaging the attention of the maritime powers of the world. Under the appropriation made by Congress, the department, on the favorable report of the board, has contracted for the construction of three iron-clad ships of different models, the aggregate cost of which will be within the limits of the appropriation. The difficulty of combining the two qualities of light draught and iron armor, both of which are wanted for service on our coast, could not be entirely overcome; but the board, in this new branch of naval architecture, has, I think, displayed great practical wisdom, and I refer to their very full and able report, which is appended, for a more explicit and detailed exhibit of their inquiries and conclusions.

STEVENS'S BATTERY.

In pursuance of the joint resolution of Congress approved June 24, 1861, authorizing the Secretary of the Navy to appoint a board to examine the iron steam battery now building at Hoboken, New Jersey, and ascertain what will be the cost of completing the same, how soon it can be completed, and the expediency thereof, I appointed Commodores Silas H. Stringham and William Inman, Captain T. A. Dornin, Chief Engineer A. C. Stimers, and Joseph Henry, Esq., Secretary of the Smithsonian Institution, a commission, and directed them to assemble on the 1st of November to prosecute the examination. The department has information that the board convened, but has as yet received no report of its proceedings.

INCREASING THE EFFICIENCY OF THE NAVY.

The efficiency of the navy may unquestionably be largely increased by creating more grades, and I would recommend that the permanent organization of the line officers be as follows :

Flag officer—to command squadrons.

Commodore,
Captain,
Commander,   } To command single ships.
Lieutenant commander,
Lieutenant.
Master.
Passed midshipman.
Midshipman.
Cadet.

The lieutenant commanders, a grade used during the revolution, may be employed as first lieutenants, and in the command of the smaller class of naval vessels.

The present rate of pay may be so apportioned among the different grades that in the aggregate there shall be no increase. Let no officer be advanced to any grade above that of passed midshipman except upon nomination of the President and confirmation by the Senate, after a board of officers shall have pronounced him morally, physically, and professionally competent to perform all his duties, both ashore and afloat.

The public service would also be promoted were some limit of age fixed by law for active service. I would, therefore, respectfully suggest that line officers be retired after having been forty-five years in the navy, excepting when called into active service by special appointment from the President. A generous pecuniary provision should be made for those who are retired after long and faithful service.

To satisfy the immediate demands of the public service, I recommend that a grade to be designated flag officer be established, and that the President, by selection from the present list of captains and commanders, appoint a number not exceeding seven, who shall each have command, irrespective of seniority or rank, of the squadron to which he may be assigned, and the appointment shall cease when the officer hauls down his flag, unless for distinguished and meritorious conduct in battle, as flag officer, he receives, upon recommendation of the President, the thanks of Congress.

RETIRING BOARDS.

Under the provisions of an act authorizing a naval retiring board, entitled "An act providing for the better organization of the military establishment," approved August 3, 1861, a board has been assembled, and is composed of Commodore George W. Storer, president; Commodore Charles H. Bell, Captain D. G. Farragut, Surgeons Charles Chase and L. B. Hunter, members; and Philip Hamilton, Esq., judge advocate. The board convened at Brooklyn on the 18th of October last, and is still prosecuting its duties.

A like board assembled at the same place on the 6th of November, under authorization by the same law, for retiring such marine officers as have become incapable of performing the duties of their office. This board is composed of Colonel John Harris, commandant of the corps, president; Brevet Major Jacob Zeilin, Major William B. Slack, Surgeons Solomon Sharp, and Charles D. Maxwell, members; and P. T. Woodbury, Esq., judge advocate.

Availing themselves of the provisions of the act referred to, several officers of the navy and of the marine corps have, upon their own application, been placed on the list of retired officers, after having been forty years in the service of the United States.

ACTING APPOINTMENTS.

In my report at the commencement of the special session I made mention of the fact that the appointment of acting lieutenants had been conferred on certain gentlemen who had retired from the navy in peaceful times, but who, when the flag was assailed, promptly tendered their services in its defence. It was not within the power of the department to restore these gentlemen to the line of promotion, but they were placed in the position of, and assigned to duty as, acting lieutenants, where they have rendered good service, and proved themselves worthy of their profession whenever they have had an opportunity, either at Hatteras, Port Royal, the Gulf, or elsewhere. There are fifteen of these formerly naval officers who have received the appointment of acting lieutenants. The question of full restoration to these gallant officers, whose names are untarnished, and who have acquitted themselves with honor to their profession, is one of interest to themselves and the country.

In pursuance of the policy indicated by Congress at the extra session, there have been appointed from the commercial marine twenty-five acting volunteer lieutenants. Great care has been exercised in the selection of these officers, who, beside their general reputation for nautical skill, have undergone an examination as to their fitness and qualifications by a board constituted for that purpose.

There have also been appointed for active service in the navy, independent of officers of the line, four hundred and thirty-three acting-masters, and two hundred and nine master's mates. All of these masters have had sea experience, and nearly every one has been a successful navigator and commander in the merchant service. It was soon found necessary also to require that master's mates should have previous sea experience to qualify them for appointment. In order to prepare the different classes of officers introduced from the mercantile marine for duty in the naval service, schools for gunnery and proper training were established at the navy yards, where the appointees have been drilled and disciplined for navy duty. The officers thus selected are, with scarcely an exception, highly meritorious, and would be a credit to any service. Composed as they are of the best material in the best commercial marine on the globe, the spirit and zeal with which they surrender their more peaceful pursuits for the severe and rigid discipline of the navy does honor to their country and themselves.

The assistant paymasters authorized to be appointed by the act of July last have been selected, but the increase of thirty-six was insufficient for the service with the large addition of vessels and crews that have been ordered. I have therefore been compelled to make further appointments of acting assistant paymasters, of whom there are now sixty-one on duty. Their appointments are temporary, for the cruise or the war, and made when there are no unemployed paymasters or assistant paymasters of the regular corps who can be detailed for the duty required.

Acting appointments of engineers and assistant engineers and of assistant surgeons have necessarily been made, in addition to the regular corps, to meet the new and extraordinary demands of the service. There has been an aggregate of nine hundred and ninety-three acting appointments for temporary service made by the department since the present difficulties commenced. That there may in some instances have been improper selections in consequence of improper recommendations is not improbable, but such are exceptional cases. In some instances men possessing high and excellent traits in other respects have been found addicted to intemperance. This is a disqualification in any officer, and whenever this habit has been detected there has been no hesitation in revoking at once the appointment.

MARINE CORPS.

The report of the commandant of the marine corps is herewith transmitted. Under the provisions of the act of March 3, 1849, with your approval, orders were given in April and May to enlist 1,152 additional non-commissioned officers and privates, to meet the requirements of the service. A large number of able-bodied men of a superior class were very readily obtained, and the increased demand for guards for vessels has rendered necessary an additional increase of five hundred privates, with the necessary non-commissioned officers, which number you have recently authorized to be enlisted.   A general return of the corps for October accompanies the report, of the commandant and shows the actual strength of the corps, ashore and afloat, to have been at that time two thousand nine hundred and sixty-four.

In July last, a battalion of 12 officers and 336 men, under Major J. G. Reynolds, was detailed for duty with the army of the Potomac, under General McDowell.   They were in the engagement at Bull Run, and Major Reynolds's report thereof will be found herewith. A similar battalion of 19 officers and 330 men, under the same officer, was despatched with the expedition to Port Royal.

NAVAL SCHOOL.

Temporary accommodations for the Naval School have been provided, and the officers and students made comfortable at Newport, where the institution was located upon its removal from Annapolis, until Congress shall take some order on the subject of its future permanent location.   Much of the public property appertaining to the school was hastily removed, but many conveniences and much that is essential were left at Annapolis, where they still remain in charge of a person to whose custody they were committed.   No legislation was consummated at the extra session towards filling up the school to its full complement in consequence of disagreement between the two houses as to the method of appointment, although each branch expressed an opinion that the deficiency ought to be supplied.

I would respectfully renew the recommendations and suggestions made in my former report, not only that the deficiency should be supplied, but that for a period, at least, the number should be largely increased.   In regard to the selection of students when representatives neglect or refuse to make the nominations, or when a district omits to elect a representative, it is suggested that the President or the Secretary of the Navy be authorized to perform that duty.

The institution is one of too great national importance to be neglected.   It is there that the youth are to be educated who in the future must maintain and elevate the character of the navy.   I have deemed it important that the accomplished superintendent, whose fidelity to his trust was exhibited under trying circumstances, should be continued in the position he has filled so acceptably until the school shall be again permanently established.   But, even under the disadvantage of a temporary location, the country should avail itself of the opportunity to educate, for a period at least, double the number now authorized by law.

EMPLOYMENT OF FUGITIVES.

In the coastwise and blockading duties of the navy it has been not unfrequent that fugitives from insurrectionary places have sought our ships for refuge and protection, and our naval commanders have applied to me for instruction as to the proper disposition which should be made of such refugees.   My answer has been that, if insurgents, they should be handed over to the custody of the government; but if, on the contrary, they were free from any voluntary participation in the rebellion and sought the shelter and protection of our flag, then they should be cared for and employed in some useful manner, and might be enlisted to serve on our public vessels or in our navy yards, receiving wages for their labor.   If such employment could not be furnished to all by the navy, they might be referred to the army, and if no employment could be found for them in the public service they should be allowed to proceed freely and peaceably without restraint to seek a livelihood in any loyal portion of the country.   This I have considered to be the whole required duty, in the premises, of our naval officers.

NAVAL DEPOT ON THE LAKES.

I have been desired to invite attention to the fact that there is no naval depot on the lakes, notwithstanding the vast amount of tonnage on that frontier, and to state that if there were one and the ability to arm the merchant marine, our rights on the lakes would be made secure.

CAPTURE OF SLAVER.

There has been but one vessel seized by the African squadron for being engaged in the slave trade since those mentioned in the last report of this department, the American brig Triton, by the United States ship Constellation, in the Congo river, on the 20th of May last.   She arrived at New York on the 10th of July, in charge of Midshipman G. A. Borchert, and was turned over to the United States marshal.

THE BUREAUS.

The reports of the chiefs of the respective bureaus attached to this department present the condition of affairs coming under their cognizance in detail.   Their labors and responsibilities have been greatly increased by the events that have occurred during the present year, but their duties have been discharged with ability and fidelity to the government, and that, too, in many respects, under peculiar disadvantages.

The navy yards at Norfolk and Pensacola, being in the hands of the insurgents, the chief of the Bureau of Yards and Docks has not had them under his supervision but for a small portion of the year.   His labors, however, have not been diminished or less arduous in consequence.

At no period since its establishment has the Bureau of Construction had so great an amount of labor devolved upon it as during the current year.   Not only the design and construction of the large number of vessels ordered to be built, but the repair and equipment of all that have been put in commission, with other attending duties, have come under the cognizance of the chief of that bureau and received his unremitting attention.

The emergency has put in requisition the energy and talent attached to the Ordnance Bureau, which, under many embarrassments, has met the demand upon it, and if, at the commencement of our difficulties, the wants of the government could not, in all instances, be supplied with the rifled cannon and Dahlgren heavy ordnance, that branch of the service is now furnishing guns and munitions with a rapidity and of a description unsurpassed in any service. The occasion is such as to stimulate into greater activity the inventive faculties and powers of the distinguished commandant of the Washington yard, whose services are as valuable to the country, and entitled to as high regard, as those of the most successful flag officer who commands a squadron. For more specific details I would refer you to the report of the Ordnance Bureau.

Most of the contracts in the Bureau of Provisions and Clothing were made on the basis of a force not exceeding 8,500 men in actual service, but the greatly increased numbers and the enhanced prices of many articles have been attended with serious consequences to the contractors, some of whom have been unable to fulfil their engagements. I am happy to say, however, that the vigilant chief of that bureau has permitted none of our squadrons to be deficient in consequence of these failures.

The affairs of the Bureau of Medicine and Surgery have been further systematized and improved under the judicious management of its intelligent chief. Like every other branch of the service, the medical staff has been largely increased, not only in the regular corps but by acting appointments.

The action of the several bureaus has been eminently satisfactory under the circumstances of the period. That the organization of the department might be modified, and an improved distribution and classification of the duties that legitimately belong to it be made, I have no doubt. Some of these have been heretofore suggested by my predecessors, and are referred to by me at this time with deference, but with a sincere conviction that more systematic efficiency might thereby be produced.

ESTIMATES AND APPROPRIATIONS.

The amount appropriated at the last regular session of Congress for the naval service for the current year was $13,168,675 86. To this was added at the special session in July last $30,446,875 91—making for the fiscal year ending June 30, 1862, an aggregate of $43,615,551 77. This sum will not be sufficient, however, for the purpose, and therefore additional appropriations will be necessary. There will be required to pay for vessels purchased, and for necessary alterations incurred in fitting them for naval purposes, the sum of $2,530,000; for the purchase of additional vessels, $2,000,000; and for the construction and completion of twenty iron-clad vessels, $12,000,000—making a total of $16,530,000. This sum is independent of the estimates submitted for the next fiscal year, and being required for current expenses as well as objects of immediate importance, it is desirable should receive early attention from Congress.

The estimates submitted by this department for the fiscal year ending June 30, 1863, amount to $44,625,665 02, viz:

For the navy proper $41,096,530 25
For the marine corps 1,105,656 77
For navy yards, hospitals, magazines, and miscellaneous objects 2,423,478 00

The reports of the chiefs of the bureaus and the commandant of the marine corps, with their accompanying estimates, exhibit in detail the objects for which the appropriations are required. I would also refer to these reports as containing information and suggestions in regard to matters pertaining to the several departments of the naval service.

CONCLUSION.

In concluding this report, it gives me pleasure to acknowledge the important aid I have received in the administration of the department from the zealous and very efficient co-operation of the Assistant Secretary and the clerical force of the department proper, and from the Chiefs of the several bureaus, and those performing public duty under their immediate superintendence and direction.

To the patriotic officers of the navy, and the brave men who, in various scenes of naval action have served under them, the department and the government justly owe an acknowledgment even more earnest and emphatic. Courage, ability, unfaltering fidelity, and devotion to the cause of their country, have been the general and noble characteristics of their conduct in the arduous and important service with which they have been intrusted. I state with all confidence that in their hands the historic renown of the American navy has been elevated and augmented. In this convulsive crisis of our country the duties of this department have been new and heavy, and its responsibilities great. I have met them all with entire honesty of purpose, and have labored assiduously and faithfully to discharge them. The result of my labors I respectfully submit to you, and through you to the judgment of Congress and the country.

GIDEON WELLES,
Secretary of the Navy.

To the President.

REPORT

OF

THE POSTMASTER GENERAL.

POST OFFICE DEPARTMENT,
December 2, 1861.

SIR: Respecting the operations and condition of this department, during the past fiscal year, ending June 30, 1861, I have the honor to report as follows:

APPOINTMENT OFFICE.

The operations of the appointment office, for the year ending June 30, 1861, show the following result:

The whole number of post offices in operation on the 30th June, 1860, was 28,498.

The whole number on the 30th June, 1861, was 28,586.

The net increase of post offices during the year ending the 30th June, 1861, is 88.

The total number of post offices at which appointments are made by the President of the United States, on the 30th June, 1861, was 434.

The table (No. 1) annexed to this report shows the number of each class of offices in the several States and Territories of the Union.

The whole number of cases acted upon during the last official year, including the appointments ordered by the President of the United States, was 10,638. The whole number of appointments made by the department during that year for all causes was 9,235. The number of appointments ordered by the President during the same period was 337. The classification of these changes by States will appear in the table (No. 2,) and a summary of them in the table (No. 3,) annexed to this report.

The whole number of post offices in operation in the United States on the 1st day of December, 1861, excluding those discontinued by special order, and including those suspended by the general orders of May and June last, was 28,620.

SPECIAL AGENTS, ROUTE AGENTS, AND LOCAL AGENTS.

The number of special agents in the employment of the department on the 30th of June last was sixteen. The extraordinary condition of the country and the exigencies of the service in certain States rendered it necessary to increase this number, up to the present time, to twenty.

During the last fiscal year the number of route agents in the service was four hundred and seventy-four, at an annual cost of $372,240.

The number of local agents was forty, at an annual cost of $25,479.

At the close of the year, on the 30th of June last, the number of route agents was reduced to three hundred and ninety-two, at a cost of $294,460.

The number of local agents was reduced to thirty-five, at a cost of $19,719.

These agents are paid salaries generally ranging from four to eight hundred dollars per annum, and from the large proportion of railroad transportation have become an important and indispensable branch of the service in distributing and despatching the mails. The special agents are the eyes and hands of the department, to detect and arrest violators of the law, and to render the mails a safe and rapid means of communication. In their selection I have endeavored to secure the qualities of integrity, sagacity, and efficiency. While the duties of route agents are different, they are always of greater importance and more onerous than is commonly apprehended, and require, to a great degree, the qualities of character above described.

FOREIGN MAIL SERVICE.

The aggregate amount of postage (sea, inland, and foreign) on mails exchanged with the United Kingdom was	$786,274 67
Do · · · · · · · · · · · · · · · · do · · · · · · · · · · · · · · · · Prussia · · ·	266,275 38
Do · · · · · · · · · · · · · · · · do · · · · · · · · · · · · · · · · France · · · ·	220,394 31
Do · · · · · · · · · · · · · · · · do · · · · · · · · · · · · · · · · Hamburg · ·	41,260 95
Do · · · · · · · · · · · · · · · · do · · · · · · · · · · · · · · · · Bremen · · ·	36,943 29
Do · · · · · · · · · · · · · · · · do · · · · · · · · · · · · · · · · Belgium · · ·	10,888 10
Total postages on European mails · · · · · · · · · ·	1,362,036 70
Being a decrease from the amount reported for the preceding year of ·	$14,365 55

The sea conveyance of these mails was performed as follows, viz:

By United States mail packets.

Of the New York and Havre Steamship Company	$105,057	58
Of Vanderbilt's European line	56,894	16
Of the North Atlantic Steamship Company	41,706	25
Total	$203,657	99

By foreign steamers employed as United States packets.

Of the Canadian line	$169,803	42
Of the Liverpool and New York and Philadelphia Steamship Company	131,071	51
Of the North German Lloyd Company	112,748	18
Of the New York and Hamburg Steamship Company	65,761	00
Total	479,384	11

By British contract mail packets.

Of the Cunard line	$650,310	81
Of the Galway line	28,683	79
Total	678,994	60
	1,362,036	70

Of this amount $814,444 39 was collected in the United States, and $547,592 31 in the United Kingdom, Prussia, France, Hamburg, Bremen and Belgium.

Excess of collections in the United States, $266,852 08.

The cost of collecting which, in commissions at United States post offices, at an estimated average of 40 per cent., would amount to $106,740 83.

The number of letters and newspapers exchanged in the mails between this country and Europe was as follows:

Letters sent from the United States	3,086,121
Letters received from Europe	3,059,700
Total	6,145,821

Newspapers sent from the United States	2,484,357
Newspapers received from Europe	1,033,633
Total	3,517,990

It appears that the number of letters sent to Europe exceeds the number received from Europe by 26,421.

The excess in the number of papers sent from the United States over those received from Europe is 1,450,724.

The amount of letter postage on mails *sent* to Great Britain was $375,754 36; to Prussia, $141,612 07; to France, $106,469 92; to Hamburg, $27,089 04 ; to Bremen, $19,713 31; and to Belgium, $5,358 59. *Total sent*, $675,997 29.

On mails *received*, from Great Britain, $410,520 31; from Prussia, $124,663 31; from France, $113,924 39; from Hamburg, $14,171 91; from Bremen, $17,229 98; and from Belgium, $5,529 51. *Total received*, $686,039 41.

The excess of postage on mails *sent* from the United States to different countries of Europe over that accruing on mails received from the same countries was as follows:

Prussia ·	$16,948 76
Hamburg ·	12,917 13
Bremen ·	2,483 33
Total ·	$32,349 22

The excess of postages accruing on mails *received* over those *sent* was as follows:

Great Britain ·	$34,765 95
France ·	7,454 47
Belgium ·	170 92
Total ·	$42,391 34

The weight of *closed letter* mails was as follows: Prussian closed mails *received*, 133,774½ ounces; *sent*, 149,572½ ounces. Total, 283,347 ounces. British closed mails for Canada, 42,058½ ounces; Canada closed mails for Great Britain, 25,000½ ounces. Total, 67,059 ounces. British and California closed mails *received*, 24,328½ ounces; *sent*, 6,412¼ ounces. Total, 30,741¼ ounces. British closed mails for Havana, 8,922½ ounces. British closed mails for Mexico, 824½ ounces.

The amount paid Great Britain for the sea and territorial transit of United States and Prussian closed mails through the United Kingdom, was $121,408 55½; and the amount received from Great Britain, for the sea and territorial transit of British closed mails through the United States, was $38,322 53½.

Balance due Great Britain, on adjustment of accounts, for the year ending June 30, 1861 ·	$149,935 24½
Balance due to France, (first, second, and third quarters, 1860) ·	24,782 13
Balance due to Prussia, for the year ending June 30, 1860 ·	41,252 47
Balance due to Bremen ·	18,073 13½

Balance due to Hamburg $15,749 63¾
Balance due the United States, on adjustment of accounts with Belgium, for the first, second, third,
and fourth quarters of 1860, and first quarter of
1861 ....   5,159 71

The amounts paid to the different lines of transatlantic steamships
employed by this department, for service performed during the year,
under the provisions of the existing law, which limits the compensation to the sea and inland postages on the mails transported, if the
conveyance is by an American steamer, and to sea postage only, if
by a foreign steamer, will appear by the table (No 4) annexed to this
report. The total cost of this service was $392,887 63. Of this
amount, $157,174 09 was earned by American steamers, performing
23 round trips, at the sea and United States inland postages, and
$235,713 54 by foreign steamers, performing 86 round trips, at the
sea postage only.

The aggregate amount of postages on the mails exchanged between
the United States and the British North American provinces during
the year was $186,900 50; of which $96,304 07 was collected in
this country, and $90,596 43 in the British provinces.

The United States postages on the West India mails was $59,544 48;
all of which has been paid to the different lines of American steamships conveying the mails to and from Havana, Matanzas, and St.
Thomas, respectively.

The United States postages on mails forwarded to, and received
from Vera Cruz, Mexico, amounted to $4,370 08, which has been,
in like manner, paid to the steamers and sailing vessels performing
the sea transportation between New Orleans and Vera Cruz.

The United States postages on the correspondence forwarded to
and received from Central and South America, and Acapulco, (Mexico,)
by the California line of steamers, via Panama, during the year,
amounted to $12,100 35. The entire California mail service was
transferred from the Isthmus to the overland route on the 1st of July
last; but the Isthmus, Central and South American mails are still
conveyed by the California line of steamers, under the existing law,
which limits the compensation to the United States postages on the
mails transported, Cornelius Vanderbilt, esq., the proprietor of the
line, having consented ''to carry them for the postages until Congress
meets, and has the opportunity of making some more permanent provision.'' It is claimed by him that the postages on these mails fall
far short of a fair and proper remuneration for the service performed
in their transportation. In view of the importance of keeping up a
direct mail communication with the Isthmus of Panama, and the
countries on the Pacific coast of Central and South America, I respectfully recommend the subject to the early consideration of Congress.

Additional articles to the United States and French postal convention of the 2d March, 1857, have been mutually agreed upon, establishing new exchanging offices, on the side of the United States, at
Portland, Detroit, and Chicago, respectively; and on the side of

France, at Paris; and providing for an exchange of mails by the Canadian mail packets plying between Liverpool and Portland, or between Liverpool and River du Loup; a copy of these articles accompanies this report, (No. 5.) Additional articles to the postal convention with Prussia, of the same character, have also been agreed upon with the general post office at Berlin, establishing, on the part of the United States, new offices of exchange at Portland, Detroit, and Chicago, respectively; to exchange closed mails with Aachen, (Aix-la-Chapelle,) through England, by means of the Canadian line of mail packets, a copy of which is annexed to this report, (No. 6.) These arrangements have greatly expedited the transmission of European correspondence to and from the western States, and give entire satisfaction to that portion of the country.

I have had the satisfaction of arranging the terms of a postal convention with Mexico, which was concluded with the Mexican minister on the 31st of July last, subject to ratification, within six months from that date, by the President of the United States by and with the advice and consent of the Senate, and by the President of the republic of Mexico with the approval of the Mexican congress. This convention was approved by the Senate of the United States on the 6th of August last; but no official information has yet been received of the action of Mexico thereupon. Its principal provisions are:

1st. The establishment of direct mail steamship service between New York and Vera Cruz, either direct or via Havana, the expense of which is to be borne equally by the respective post departments of the two countries.

2d. A uniform rate of postage between the two countries of 25 cents for a single letter under half an ounce in weight, and an additional charge of 25 cents for each additional fraction of half an ounce; pre-payment of which is obligatory and each country to retain all the postage it collects, which dispenses entirely with any postage accounts between the two countries.

3d. With respect to printed matter of every kind, each country is to levy and collect its own postage only at the established domestic rates, and the despatching country is to charge and collect, in addition to its regular domestic inland rate, a sea rate of one cent on each newspaper, and one cent per ounce on pamphlets and other kinds of printed matter.

4th. Each country grants to the other the territorial transit of closed mail bags through its territories, free from all duties, tax, detention, or examination; the means of transporting such bags to be furnished, and the cost thereof to be paid, by the country to which they may respectively belong; and the carriages, cattle, and men, exclusively employed in the service, to be free from arrest, charges, or molestation of any kind whatever, except for some flagrant violation of the laws of the country through which the closed bags are conveyed.

If this convention should be ratified by Mexico, special legislation will be necessary to provide for the portion of the expenses to be paid by this department in maintaining a regular line of mail packets between New York and Vera Cruz; as the provisions of the existing laws limit the compensation for sea service to the postages, which will be wholly inadequate to sustain such a line of packets.

A special appropriation from the treasury will be required to enable the Postmaster General to carry this convention into operation. It is not only important as a postal arrangement, in view of the present interruption of mail communication *via* New Orleans, but it is also regarded as a measure of great political and commercial importance to the respective countries.

Propositions have been submitted for postal arrangements with the governments of Costa Rica and Guatemala, respectively, which are now under consideration; and the department has other arrangements in contemplation for improvements in our postal intercourse with foreign countries by the reduction of rates of postage and increased certainty and efficiency in the transportation of the mails.

The negotiations with the British office for a reduction of postage, which have been pending since 1857, were unsuccessful, chiefly, as I understand it, because of the difference of the offices as to whether the steamers employed should receive a greater or less proportion of the postage remaining, after deducting the United States inland rate of three cents. This point did not seem to me to be of sufficient significance to be allowed to defeat a measure of so much importance to the commerce of both countries as the reduction of 50 per cent. of the rate of postage. Although fully concurring with my predecessors that the basis proposed by this department was the more just as it recognized and was founded upon the inland rates established by the laws of the two countries, I have, on a review of the whole subject, concluded to accept the division of rates as proposed, which grants to the United Kingdom the same rate of inland postage, rather than longer delay an arrangement so desirable as that sought to be attained by the proposed reduction of the international letter postage from 24 to 12 cents the single rate. I have, therefore, formally accepted the basis for international letters as originally proposed by the British office on the 13th of February, 1857, that the benefit of the reduction may accrue to the written correspondence between the two countries as early as practicable. The other propositions relating to printed matter and territorial transit charges are held for further consideration and arrangement as soon as the respective departments find it practicable to give them attention. I trust that a review of these subjects, by the respective postal administrations, may result in further advantages to the people engaged in this intercourse.

MEXICAN MAILS ON THE PACIFIC COAST.

I commend to the consideration of Congress the propriety of an appropriation to sustain a reliable mail communication on the coast between San Francisco and the several ports of the Mexican republic on the Pacific.

6 M

CONTRACT OFFICE—TRANSPORTATION STATISTICS.

In consequence of the defection of the insurrectionary States, and the termination of the mail service in those States on the 31st of May last, under the act of Congress approved February 28, 1861, (with the exception of service in Western Virginia,) it becomes necessary to present the transportation statistics in two divisions. These are shown in tables A and B attached to this report.

Table A exhibits the service as it stood on the 30th of June last in the States of Maine, New Hampshire, Vermont, Massachusetts, Rhode Island, Connecticut, New York, New Jersey, Pennsylvania, Delaware, Maryland, Ohio, Western Virginia, Michigan, Indiana, Illinois, Wisconsin, Iowa, Missouri, Minnesota, Kentucky, Tennessee, California, Oregon, and Kansas, and the Territories of New Mexico, Utah, Nebraska, and Washington, at which time there were in operation in those States and Territories 6,340 mail-routes, the number of contractors being 5,644. The length of these routes was 140,399 miles, and the mode of service divided as follows, viz:

Railroad	22,018
Steamboat	5,339
Coach	30,733
Inferior	82,309

The annual transportation of mails was 54,455,454 miles, costing $5,309,454, divided as follows, viz:

Railroad	23,116,823 miles, at	$2,543,709,	about	11	cents a mile.
Steamboat	1,830,016	"	290,559,	"	15⅞	"	"
Coach	10,655,783	"	1,171,295,	"	11	"	"
Inferior modes,	18,852,832	"	1,303,891,	"	7	"	"

The number of route agents in the service was 392, at a compensation of	$294,460 00
The number of local agents was 35, costing	19,719 00
The number of mail messengers was 1,532, costing	188,936 89
The number of railroad baggage masters in charge of the express mails was 48, costing	5,760 00
	$508,875 89
This sum, added to the cost of service in operation on the 30th of June	5,309,508 00
Makes the total on the 30th of June last	$5,818,383 89

The lettings of new contracts for the term commencing July 1, 1861, and ending June 30, 1865, embrace the routes in the States of Maine, New Hampshire, Vermont, Massachusetts, Rhode Island,

Connecticut, and New York, and the following shows the service under those lettings for the first quarter of the contract year ended 30th of September last:

Railroad..........	6,546 miles,	7,553,070 miles annual transportation,		$753,814 cost
Steamboat........	463 "	283,362 " "	"	16,463 "
With "celerity, certainty, and security".....	16,533 "	5,964,562 " "	"	263,730 "
	23,542	13,800,994		$1,034007

Compared with the service on the 30th June last the length of routes is diminished fifty-seven miles; but from the increase of trips, especially upon railroads, the annual transportation is increased 447,178 miles, and the cost, $24,154.

Table B shows the length of routes in the States of Virginia, (exclusive of Western Virginia,) North Carolina, South'Carolina, Georgia, Florida, Alabama, Mississippi, Arkansas, Louisiana, and Texas, on the 31st of May last, to have been 96,015 miles, divided as follows :

Railroad	6,886
Steamboat...	7,716
Coach	12,711
Inferior modes............	68,702

The total annual transportation was 24,122,711 miles, as follows :

Railroad..............	5,701,093 miles, at	$978,910	
Steamboat	1,721,850 "	574,699	
Coach	4,769,740 "	824,393	
Inferior modes.........	11,930,028 "	863,179	
			$3,241,181
To which add 121 route agents, costing......		86,400	
7 local agents.............................		3,760	
180 mail messengers.......................		28,115	
			118,275
Making the total cost of the service in those States, discontinued on the 31st of May......................			3,359,456
To this add the cost of the service in Tennessee as it stood on June 30, 1861...............................			250,232
Also the amount of compensation to route agents at the same date.....................................			12,300
Local agents			1,000
Mail messengers			3,739
			26,727

OVERLAND CALIFORNIA MAIL.

By the 9th section of an act of Congress approved March 2, 1861, entitled "An act making appropriations for the service of the Post Office Department during the fiscal year ending June 30, 1862," authority is given to the Postmaster General to discontinue the mail service on the southern overland route, (known as the "Butterfield" route,) between St. Louis and Memphis and San Francisco, and to provide for the conveyance, by the same parties, of a six times a week mail by the "central route;" that is, "from some point on the Missouri river, connecting with the east, to Placerville, California." In pursuance of this act, and the acceptance of its terms by the mail company, an order was made on the 12th of March, 1861, to modify the present contract, so as to discontinue service on the southern route, and to provide for the transportation of the entire letter mail six times a week on the central route, to be carried through in twenty days eight months in the year, and in twenty-three days four months in the year, from St. Joseph, Missouri, (or Atchison, Kansas,) to Placerville, and also to convey the entire mail three times a week to Denver City and Salt Lake; the entire letter mail to California to be carried, whatever may be its weight, and in case it should not amount to 600 pounds, then sufficient of other mail to be carried each trip to make up that weight, the residue of all mail matter to be conveyed in thirty-five days, with the privilege of sending it from New York to San Francisco in twenty-five days by sea, and the public documents in thirty-five days; a pony express to be run twice a week until the completion of the overland telegraph, through in ten days eight months, and twelve days four months, in the year, conveying for the government, free of charge, five pounds of mail matter; the compensation for the whole service to be one million of dollars per annum, payable from the general treasury, as provided by the act; the service to commence July 1, 1861, and terminate July 1, 1864. The transfer of stock from the southern to the central route was commenced about the 1st of April, and was completed so that the first mail was started from St. Joseph on the day prescribed by the order, July 1, 1861, While the carriages have, it is believed, departed regularly since that time, the mail service has not been entirely satisfactory to the department. The causes of complaint, however, it is hoped will be removed by the measures now in progress. The route selected is that by Salt Lake City, so that that office has now the advantage of a daily mail, and Denver City is supplied three times a week. The overland telegraph having been completed, the running of the pony express was discontinued October 26, 1861. By the terms of the law the contractors were required to convey only the California letter mail on each trip by the short schedule, and this they were to do whatever might be its weight; but by voluntary agreement they stipulated that in case it should fall short of 600 pounds on any occasion they would take other mails so as to make that weight. As the letter mails are seldom or never equal to

600 pounds in weight some papers are conveyed in connexion with the letter mails each trip by the short schedule, while others are necessarily delayed. This has occasioned complaint, and complaints have also been made of other delays, and that bags of printed matter have been thrown off *en route* for the admission of passengers and express matter. These charges are denied by the contractors; but while the conditions of the contract, fixed by law, allow a longer time for the transit of some mails than others, complaint and disappointment must of necessity occur.

At the commencement of threatening disturbances in Missouri, in order to secure this great daily route from interruption I ordered the increase of the weekly and tri-weekly service then existing between Omaha and Fort Kearney to daily, and an increase of pay thereon of $14,000 per annum. By that means an alternative and certain daily route between the east and California was obtained through Iowa, by which the overland mails have been transported when they became unsafe on the railroad route in Missouri.

In sending them from Davenport, through the State of Iowa, joining the main route at Fort Kearney, in Kansas, the only inconvenience experienced was a slight delay, no mails being lost so far as known.

NEW YORK AND BOSTON NIGHT MAIL.

This important addition to the facilities for conveying correspondence between these cities, announced in the last annual report as having been commenced as a three months experiment, proved to be so satisfactory and successful that the arrangement was continued with the same companies, viz.: those composing the inland line, through Hartford and Springfield, until the 1st of August last, when negotiations with those corporations failing to secure a renewal of their services, the mail was transferred to the "shore line," from New Haven, through New London, Stonington, and Providence, over which line it is now carried with great regularity, and much to the satisfaction of the citizens interested and of the department.

NIGHT MAIL FROM NEW YORK TO WASHINGTON.

This mail leaves New York at 11 in the evening, and arrives at Washington by 9.30 the next morning. Connexions are thus made at New York with railway trains from Montreal, Ogdensburg, Buffalo, &c., arriving at 10.30 p. m., and by a recent change in the hour of departure of the express train at Boston from 3 to 2 p. m., connecting with that train also, so that mails and passengers leaving Boston at 2 p. m. arrive at Washington by 9.30 a. m., or in less than twenty-three hours.

This is about the time occupied by the other lines, but it constitutes the *third* daily direct and unbroken line of travel for mails and passengers from city to city, and at hours causing the least loss of business time.

FINANCE OFFICE.

The details of the financial operations of this department during the fiscal year ending June 30, 1861, are fully exhibited in the accompanying very elaborate and interesting report of the Auditor for this department, from which the following statement is derived:

Revenue and expenditures.

The expenditures of the department in the fiscal year ending June 30, 1861, amounted to $13,606,759 11, viz:

For transportation of inland mails, including payments to route agents, local agents, and mail messengers··		$8,406,652 51
For transportation of foreign mails, to wit:		
Between New York, Southampton, and Havre ·························	$266,549 05	
Between New York, Queenstown, and Liverpool ······················	44,733 31	
Between New York, New Orleans, and Havana···························	4,803 23	
Between New York and Havana········	37,597 64	
Between New Orleans and Havana·····	10,422 27	
Between Portland and Liverpool······	76,418 52	
		440,524 02
Between New York and San Francisco··	299,239 99	
Mails across the Isthmus of Panama····	25,000 00	
Expenses of government mail agents at Panama·······················	1,857 36	
		326,097 35
For compensation to postmasters ················		2,514,157 14
For clerks in post offices ··························		947,206 31
For ship, steamboat, and way letters··············		12,007 06
For office furniture for post offices················		2,177 55
For advertising ·································		40,752 70
For mail-bags.·································		66,966 61
For blanks ·································		79,859 18
For mail-locks, keys, and office stamps ·············		8,650 14
For mail depredations and special agents·············		47,837 22
For postage stamps and stamped envelopes ·········		92,772 70
For wrapping paper·····························		50,920 96
For payments to letter-carriers····················		149,073 62
For repayments for dead letters ·················		9 48
For interest under act of February 15, 1860 ········		4,699 54
For miscellaneous payments ····················		271,446 61
For payments for balances due on British mails······		120,507 82
For payments for balances due on French mails······		24,440 59
Actual expenditure for 1861·················		$13,606,759 11

The expenditures for the year ending June 30, 1860,
were $14,874,772 89
The expenditures for the year ending June 30, 1861,
were 13,606,759 11

Decrease in 1861 .... $1,268,013 78

The gross revenue for the year 1861, including receipts from letter carriers and from foreign postages, amounted to $8,349,296 40, as stated below:

Letter postage $646,498 14
Registered letters 19,305 66
Stamps sold 6,864,791 43
Newspapers and pamphlets 571,209 28
Fines 20 00
Receipts on account of emoluments 94,563 45
Receipts on account of letter carriers 149,073 62
Miscellaneous receipts 3,834 82

$ 8,349,296 40

The balance to the credit of the department, on the
books of the Auditor, June 30, 1860 .... $1,211,860 17
The receipts of the department from all sources during the year 1861 .... 8,349,296 40
Balance on credit accounts closed by suspense 5,902 90
Amount of various appropriations drawn from the
treasury during the year, as specifically shown by
the Auditor, was 4,645,994 40

Total receipts $14,213,053 87
The whole amount of expenses in the
year $13,606,759 11
Add amount of accounts closed by bad
debts 407 17
————————— 13,607,166 28

Leaving to the credit of the revenue account .... ·$605,887 59

The expenditure for 1861, inclusive of bad debts, and
exclusive of credit balance, on accounts closed by
suspense, as exhibited $13,601,263 38
Deduct the revenue for 1861 .... $8,349,296 40
Add the earnings of this department
in carrying free mail matter 700,000 00
————————— 9,049,296 40

Deficiency $4,551,966 98

The estimated deficiency of means for 1861, as pre-
sented in the annual report from this department,
December 3, 1859, was $5,988,424 04
Deduct actual deficiency...... .... 4,551,966 98

Excess of estimated deficiency over actual deficiencies 1,436,457 06

The revenue from all sources during the year 1860
amounted to................................. $9,218,067 40
The revenue from all sources during the year 1861
amounted to............................. 9,049,296 40

Decrease of revenue for 1861.............. 168,771 00

*Statement of gross and net proceeds from post offices in the loyal and
disloyal States, for the fiscal years ending June 30, 1860, and 1861.*

LOYAL STATES.

Year.	Gross proceeds.	Compensation to post-masters and incidental expenses.	Net proceeds.
1860................	$6,692,012 25	$3,003,321 69	$3,688,690 56
1861................	6,890,097 20	3,088,610 12	3,801,487 08
		Increase in 1861	$112,796 52

DISLOYAL STATES.

Year.	Gross proceeds.	Compensation to post-masters and incidental expenses.	Net proceeds.
1860................	$1,517,540 55	$696,994 04	$820,546 51
1861................	1,241,220 05	563,513 35	677,706 70
		Decrease in 1861....	$142,839 81

The decrease in 1861 from the net proceeds of 1860 in all the
States appears to be $30,043 29.

*Statement of the receipts and expenditures of the disloyal States, and
amount alleged to be due to contractors; also, the amount actually paid
to contractors from July 1, 1860, to May 31, 1861.*

Total expenditures $3,699,150 47
Total gross receipts 1,241,220 05

Excess of expenditures over receipts 2,457,930 42

Amount alleged to be due to contractors for transportation ···· ······ ····················· $3,135,637 12
Amount actually paid for transportation ··· ······ 2,323,061 63

Leaving amount alleged to be due and unpaid ·· $812,575 49

The tabular statement of the auditor, marked No. 3, exhibits in detail the receipts from, and the expenditures in, the post offices in all the States during the fiscal year, together with the amount paid, and reported to be due, to contractors for the transportation of the mails.

No. 4 presents a similar exhibit for the disloyal States alone, with a statement of the whole amount of "transportation" accrued therein, which includes not only the amount actually paid, but also the cost of the service known to have been performed, payment for which is withheld, and the additional amount which would be due on the assumption that the postal service was uninterrupted until discontinued by the Postmaster General.

Estimates for 1862.

The estimates of receipts and expenditures for the fiscal year ending June 30, 1862, and of the resulting deficiency for the same year, which were submitted in the last annual report from this department, were based on the existence of postal service throughout the Union.

Should such service remain suspended, during the year, in States where it is now wholly or partially discontinued, the estimated deficiency of $5,210,426 63 would be reduced to $2,747,000, according to the ratio of receipts and expenditures in that section in 1860.

The amount appropriated by the 3d section of the act approved March 2, 1861, to supply deficiencies in the revenue for the year 1862, was $5,391,350 63; and, if the cost of a daily mail on the central route is to be paid out of the resources of this department, there will be an unexpended balance of this appropriation July 1, 1863, of about $1,600,000.

Sections 9 and 11 of the act approved March 2, 1861, (chapter 73,) seemed clearly to authorize this payment out of the treasury for mail service six times a week on the central route to California. But the word "daily," used in the 11th section, in connexion with the appropriation, has induced the adoption of a different construction at the treasury.

Estimate of receipts and expenditures for 1863.

EXPENDITURES.

For transportation of the mails inland ···· ········· $6,961,000 00
For compensation of postmasters ················ 2,234,000 00
For clerks of post offices ······················ 846,000 00
For ship, steamboat, and way letters ············ 12,000 00

For office furniture for post offices...............	$2,000	00
For advertising	36,000	00
For mail bags	75,000	00
For paper for blanks	50,000	00
For printing blanks	12,000	00
For wrapping paper	45,000	00
For mail locks, keys, and stamps	56,000	00
For mail depredations and special agents	75,000	00
For miscellaneous payments	187,000	00
For postage stamps and stamped envelopes	90,000	00
For payments of balances due to foreign countries..	230,000	00
For payments of letter carriers	152,000	00
	$11,063,000	**00**

To the above estimate must be added the cost of
transportation of "foreign mails," which was formerly paid out of the appropriation of the 5th section
of the act approved June 14, 1858, but which the
Secretary of the Treasury, on the 6th of August,
1861, decided not to be payable therefrom, since the
passage of the act of June 15, 1860.

Estimate for the transportation of foreign mails for 1863.

Between New York, Southampton, and other European ports.......................................	285,000	00
Between New York, Queenstown, and Liverpool....	50,000	00
Between Portland and Liverpool, and Quebec and Liverpool.....................................	80,000	00
Between United States, Havana, Cuba, and other West India ports.............................	50,000	00
	$11,528,000	**00**

The estimate for the transportation of the mails
inland does not include the sum of $1,000,000.
which it was presumed that Congress intended to
appropriate from the treasury by the 9th section of
the act of March 2, 1861, for a daily mail on the
central route; but by a decision of the First Comp-
troller of the Treasury, dated October 31, 1861, it is
declared that this sum was not thus appropriated.
Unless, therefore, a specific appropriation for this
object be made by Congress, the above estimates
will be subject to a further addition of 1,000,000 00

Expenditures for 1863 .... 12,528,000 00

MEANS FOR 1863.

The gross revenue for the year 1863, including foreign postages, fees paid in by letter carriers, and
miscellaneous receipts, is estimated at an increase
of four per cent, on the revenues of 1861, making.. $8,683,000 00

Estimated deficiency of revenue, compared with estimated expenditure ···························· 3,845,000 00
Deduct appropriations made by the acts of March 3,
1847, and March 3, 1851, for carrying free mail
matter ································· 700,000 00

Which would make the whole amount estimated to
be required from the treasury for 1863·········· 3,145,000 00

Exclusive of the earnings of the department for carrying free matter under the acts of March 3, 1847,
and March 3, 1851 ··· ····················· $700,000 00

The estimate of the total expenditures for 1863 is somewhat less
than those for previous years heretofore submitted. This difference
arises from the fact that only partial estimates are made for the cost
of postal service in States where it is now suspended.

It is assumed that the restoration of such service in these States
will take place gradually, and that in the process many expensive
mail routes, from which but little revenue has been derived, may be
curtailed or discontinued.

Most of the estimates for expenditures in the disloyal States for
1863 are calculated at a fixed proportion of the amount expended in
that section of the country under the various heads of appropriation
while its relations to this department were undisturbed, which amount
was about one quarter of the expenditure for the whole Union.

The estimates for blanks and wrapping paper are nearly the same
as in former years, as in case of the resumption of postal service in
the disloyal States a large quantity of blanks, wrapping paper, and
other supplies furnished by blank agents would undoubtedly be
required, as the post offices within the limits of these States would
be entirely without such supplies.

For reasons stated below, there has been no diminution in the estimates for the cost of mail bags, locks and keys, for the year 1863.

Since the discontinuance of the postal service in eleven States of
the Union, the expenditure for mail bags has been greater than
during any corresponding period of the preceding year. The causes
are as follows :

1st. The abstraction in those States, immediately preceding open
rebellion, of considerable quantities of mail bags from the general
supply in circulation on the principal routes between the north and

the south, by withholding, in disregard of an established rule, the return of extra bags, which, by the course and exchanges of mail matter, always accumulate in the southern States, and by exchanging, and sending back with the mails old bags nearly unserviceable for new ones received.

2d. The vast increase of mailable matter incident to the war.

3d. The difficulty (arising from the rebellion and the exigencies of war) in procuring mail bags, made as heretofore, of cotton duck or canvas, in sufficient quantities, thereby rendering necessary the purchase to a great extent of such as are made of leather.

During the fiscal year ending 30th June, 1861, there were purchased, under contract, and put into the service 7,787 locked pouches and bags, (used for the transmission of letters,) which cost $26,697 51, being about 37 per cent. more in number, and about 75 per cent. more in cost, than the locked pouches and bags procured during the year next preceding; also, 22,964 canvas sacks, (used for the transmission of newspapers and other printed matter,) which cost $20,305 78, being slightly more in number, and about 5½ per cent. less in cost, than the canvas sacks procured during the same period.

The amount of $30,000, for mail locks and keys, would be a sufficient estimate for the wants of the mail service within its present limits only, including the cost of an entirely new issue of mail locks and keys, rendered indispensable for the safety of the mails, in consequence of the rebellion existing within a large portion of the former limits of the service, where the locks and keys of this department are still in use.

After due advertisement, I have made a contract for new locks and keys, which in respect to the quality and price of the articles to be furnished is more favorable than any hitherto made by this department.

Assuming the re-establishment of the mail service throughout the States now under insurrectionary control, the additional supply requisite to cover that extent of service will, it is believed, cost $20,000 more, making the total sum requisite in that case $50,000, as estimated.

Although the revenue of 1861, as compared with that of 1860, shows a diminution of nearly two per cent., yet it is anticipated that the revenue of 1863 will exhibit an increase of four per cent. on that of 1861, or nearly two per cent. on that of 1860. This estimate is justified by a comparison between the proceeds of the larger offices during the quarter ending September 30, 1860, and the corresponding quarter of the present year, which shows a small excess of revenue during the latter period.

In the appendix will be found a detailed statement of the annual revenues and expenditures from 1853 to 1861, inclusive, together with estimates for 1862 and 1863.

POST OFFICES.

The number of post offices in operation during the year was 28,586, and the number of quarterly returns received therefrom was 105,066.

The number of post offices in disloyal States which have made no returns for the third quarter of 1861 is 8,535. In the State of Virginia 167 offices continue to send in their quarterly accounts regularly.

DRAFTS AND WARRANTS.

The whole number of drafts and warrants issued during the year in payment of balances reported by the Auditor to be due mail contractors and other creditors of the department, was 21,977. The warrants were drawn on eighteen United States depositories, and the drafts on thirty post office depositories and postmasters at draft offices, with whom it is necessary for this purpose to keep summary cash accounts, as well as with 987 depositing offices.

At the depositories and draft offices $2,796,011 76, which is more than three-fifths of the net revenue of the department, was concentrated and disbursed during the year. The remainder was collected by mail contractors by means of orders on postmasters at "collection offices," prepared and sent out by the Auditor.

From the 11th of July to the 13th of September, thirty-one hundred and seventy-seven treasury notes, bearing six per cent. interest, and payable two years after date, were registered and paid to contractors and others. The aggregate amount of these notes was $1,016,800.

POSTAGE STAMPS AND STAMPED ENVELOPES.

The number of each denomination of postage stamps issued to postmasters during each of the four quarters of the year ending June 30, 1861, was as follows, viz:

Quarter ending—	1-cent.	3-cent.	5-cent.	10-cent.	12-cent.	24-cent.	30-cent.	90-cent.
September 30, 1860	12,756,100	36,512,700	146,920	922,150	384,800	170,000	103,860	11,960
December 31, 1860	14,778,085	39,171,800	178,640	1,154,910	243,825	201,150	105,960	6,200
March 31, 1861	14,174,768	41,922,956	223,000	852,900	232,400	147,325	65,040	4,110
June 30, 1861	12,184,839	33,615,600	128,640	995,730	192,875	132,125	65,140	2,010
Total	53,893,792	151,223,056	677,200	3,925,690	1,053,900	650,600	340,000	24,280

The number of stamped envelopes issued during the above period was as follows, viz:

Quarter ending—	3 cents, note size.	3 cents, letter size.	10 cents, letter size.	6 cents, official.	1 cent, letter size.	4 cents, letter size.	3 cents, note size, ruled.	3 cents, letter size, ruled.	1 cent, letter size, ruled.	4 cents, letter size, ruled.
September 30, 1860	189,250	5,777,950	27,750	10,250	----	----	28,450	668,750	----	----
December 31, 1860	146,050	3,763,200	15,350	14,650	594,500	35,000	40,350	1,657,750	412,000	35,000
March 31, 1861	82,150	3,657,600	50,150	5,800	536,250	----	66,350	2,541,150	627,750	----
June 30, 1861	53,900	2,456,700	38,500	9,750	403,500	----	31,800	1,778,700	271,000	----
Total	471,350	15,655,450	131,750	40,450	1,534,250	35,000	166,950	6,646,350	1,310,750	35,000

Whole number stamps, 211,788,518; value ·········· ···· $5,908,522 60
Whole number stamped envelopes, 26,027,300; value·   781,711 13

    Total amount for 1861· ···················· $6,690,233 73
Total value of postage stamps and stamped envelopes
    issued during the year ended June 30, 1860 ······   6,870,316 19

    Decrease during 1861 ··············· ···· ···· $180,082 46

The aggregate value of the envelopes included in the above statement is $781,711 13; but this sum does not give a correct idea of the
real amount of postage represented, inasmuch as it includes the cost
of the envelopes as well as the value of the stamps.

The postage represented is· ····················· ···· $734,354 50
Leaving as the cost of the envelopes and of their dis-
    tribution ······ ···· ······················   47,356 63

The above decrease in the issues of postage stamps and stamped
envelopes is contrary to all former experience, and is to be attributed
to the then anticipated interruption of mail communication with the
disloyal portion of the country, as the amount of each distributed
continued steadily to increase up to the commencement of the second
quarter of 1861, at which time orders from postmasters in that section were wholly or partially suspended. It was not deemed advisable to fill orders from postmasters in States which claimed to have
"seceded," without first ascertaining their disposition to hold themselves personally responsible for such amounts as might be sent them.
With this view, a circular was prepared, about twelve hundred copies
of which were addressed to different postmasters upon the receipt of
their orders.   Nine hundred replies were received, all but twenty of
which avowed the personal responsibility of the writers for all revenues
accruing at their respective offices, and their regret at the action of
their State authorities. ·Stamps were accordingly sent them until
June 1, when it appeared that the postal service could no longer be
safely continued.   The balance of stamps and stamped envelopes
remaining unaccounted for in the hands of postmasters in disloyal
States on the 1st of October, amounted to $207,000, without reference
to commissions and allowances which may be placed to their credit in
the future settlement of their accounts.

The total amount of postage stamps and stamped envelopes sold
during the year was· ······················· ···· $6,864,791 43
Amount used in prepayment of postage and cancelled
    was ······ ············· ·········· ···· ····   6,459,622 05

Leaving afloat and in the possession of purchasers,
    and being used to some extent as currency ······   405,169 38

The contract for the manufacture of postage stamps having expired
on the 10th of June, 1861, a new one was entered into with the
National Bank Note Company, of New York, upon terms very advan-

tageous to the department, from which there will result an annual saving of more than thirty per cent. in the cost of the stamps.

In order to prevent the fraudulent use of the large quantity of stamps remaining unaccounted for in the hands of postmasters in the disloyal States, it was deemed advisable to change the design and the color of those manufactured under the new contract, and also to modify the stamp upon the stamped envelopes, and to substitute, as soon as possible, the new for the old issue. It was the design of the department that the distribution of the new stamps and envelopes should commence on the first of August, but, from unavoidable delays, that of the latter did not take place until the 15th of that month.

The number of postage stamps of the new style issued up to the 9th of November was 77,117,520, and the number of new stamped envelopes 8,939,650. All post offices in the loyal States, with the exception of certain offices in Kentucky and Missouri, have been supplied therewith. Those of the old issue have been exchanged and superseded. The old stamps on hand, and such as were received by exchange, at the larger offices, have been to a great extent counted and destroyed, and those at the smaller offices returned to the department. It is proper to state that, in anticipation of the substitution of the new stamps and envelopes for the old issue, but limited supplies of the latter were sent to postmasters during June and July, so that the amount thereof remaining in their hands was comparatively small.

The additional expense incurred by the change is very inconsiderable, in view of the greatly diminished cost of the new stamps as compared with that of the old, while the prevention thereby of the use of stamps unaccounted for in the hands of disloyal postmasters saves the department from severe loss. Although the enumeration and destruction of the old stamps and envelopes is not yet completed, there is ample evidence that few received in exchange were sent from disloyal States.

Envelopes of official size, at higher rates of postage, viz: 12 cents, 24 cents, and 40 cents, have been prepared during the past year, for the purpose of mailing large packages and for foreign correspondence. The aggregate number of these issued was 20,100. Of the patent ruled envelopes, nearly 2,500,000 have been distributed to postmasters, together with 79,150 letter sheets and envelopes combined, and 186,700 newspaper wrappers. The demand for the latter has of late rapidly increased.

It is believed that a change of the present system of issuing postage stamps and envelopes would prove to be highly advantageous. Instead of being delivered, as at present, on orders from postmasters, and charged to their account, the latter might be required to purchase a sufficient quantity to meet the wants of their respective offices. This would simplify the accounts of the department, expedite the collection of its revenues, obviate losses from bad debts, and supersede the necessity of litigation for their recovery. It is, therefore, respectfully recommended to the consideration of Congress.

DEAD LETTERS.

The whole number of ordinary dead letters received and examined during the year was about 2,550,000.

The number of these letters containing money which were registered and sent out during the year ending June 30, 1861, was 10,580.

The number containing deeds, bills of exchange, drafts, and other articles of value, was 10,235.

For details, see Tables (Nos. 7 and 8) hereto appended.

There have been received and examined 125,000 letters which could not be forwarded to their destination, because of unpaid postage or carriers' fees, or because misdirected, &c. Of these there were sent out 53,934.

From the 1st of June to the 1st of November there were received at the dead letter office, in consequence of the suspension of postal communication, 76,769 letters, originating in loyal States, and addressed to residents of disloyal States. Of this number, there were returned to the writers 26,711.

During the same period 34,792 foreign letters, destined for that section, were returned as "dead," and 2,246 of them were delivered in the loyal States to authorized agents of the parties addressed, making the whole number sent out 103,886, which is considerably more than three times the quantity sent out during the previous year, when the number was unusually large.

In addition to the above, about 40,000 letters from disloyal States, addressed to parties in the loyal States, were sent to the dead letter office after the suspension of the postal service, a large proportion of which were forwarded to their destination. The last three classes are not embraced in the above enumeration of ordinary dead letters.

FOREIGN LETTERS.

The number of dead letters returned unopened to foreign countries during the fiscal year was 111,147, divided as follows:

Returned to England	58,069
Returned to France	10,088
Returned to Prussia	11,584
Returned to Hamburg	2,813
Returned to Bremen	3,302
Returned to Belgium	113
Returned to Canada	22,337
Returned to Nova Scotia	1,125
Returned to New Brunswick	1,533
Returned to Prince Edward's Island	183
Total	111,147

Which added to the number of domestic letters (103,886) sent out as above, gives the whole number sent out from the dead letter office for the year 215,033.

7 M

During the same period the sum of $53,565 90 in money, and bills of exchange, drafts, checks, and negotiable notes to the amount of $2,436,546, found in dead letters, were returned to the owners or writers thereof.

In consequence of the great accumulation, after the suspension of mail service, of letters originating in or addressed to the disloyal States, the attention of the clerical force of the dead letter office was necessarily diverted from its accustomed duties, hence the causes of the non-delivery of valuable letters were not ascertained to so great an extent as was intended, or as could be wished.

The result of successful investigation in 7,560 cases, however, confirms the past experience of the department that the failure of a letter to reach its destination is, in the vast majority of instances, the fault alone of the writer or sender. Out of the above 7,560 valuable dead letters, 3,095 were directed to the wrong office; 467 were imperfectly addressed; 612 were directed to transient persons; 257 to parties who had changed their residences; 821 were addressed to fictitious persons or firms; 83 were uncalled for; 10 without any directions; 2,136 were not mailed for want of postage stamps; 79 were missent; and for the failure of postmasters to deliver 133 no satisfactory reason was assigned. The department, therefore, can justly be held responsible for the non-delivery of but 212 of these letters.

In the examination of 110,457 letters not mailed for want of postage or carriers' fees, or because misdirected, &c., (of which number 60,231 were contributed by the offices at the twenty-four largest cities in the country,) it was found that 82,582 were detained for non-payment of postage, 6,119 for want of carrier's fee, 5,947 were misdirected, and 366 were destitute of address or direction.

Of the above letters 1,339 contained money, amounting to $7,372 50, and 1,353 checks, drafts, or negotiable paper, the value of which was $259,716 59. Letters of the last class were generally from mercantile firms or from bankers, by whom they were carelessly mailed either without the proper address or without a postage stamp.

It is worthy of remark that out of 76,769 letters, before alluded to, originating in the loyal States, and addressed to residents of disloyal States, 40,000 could not be returned, either because the signature of the writer was incomplete, or because the letter contained no clue to his residence. The experience of the department shows that a large proportion of domestic letters written by educated persons, and particularly by women, are deficient in one or both of these respects.

The 6th section of the act approved February 27, 1861, authorizes the application of the unclaimed money from dead letters to promote the efficiency of the dead letter office, by providing for a more careful examination of letters, and the return of a larger number to the writers, with or without valuable enclosures.

By virtue of the authority thus granted, from the 10th of April to the 10th of October the average number of clerks employed per month was nine, and the average compensation paid each per month was $68 52½, which, together with incidental expenses, ($21 38,) amounted to $4,544 11, leaving a balance to the credit of the dead-letter fund on the 31st of October of $755 89.

As stated above, the suspension of postal communication with the disloyal States produced an unprecedented accumulation of dead letters, which rendered the employment of these clerks in the examination, registration, and delivery of such letters an absolute necessity. It is, however, the earnest desire of the department that the dead-letter fund should be exclusively devoted to increasing the number of ordinary dead letters returned to the writers, and to insuring the utmost promptness in their delivery.

Notwithstanding the manifest advantages of the law of February 27, 1861, requiring more frequent returns of dead letters to the department, the majority of postmasters, particularly those at the smaller offices, fail to comply with the necessary regulations under that law, although duly notified thereof. In order to carry out the salutary reform contemplated by Congress, every postmaster who is delinquent in this respect is reminded of what the law requires, and his immediate compliance therewith requested. This correspondence, and the consequent return of a larger amount of letters to the owners, involves much additional labor, tending to increase the efficiency of the dead letter office.

According to the experience of the last year, it would appear that the proportion of the dead letters sent out which would be received by the writers is much larger than was formerly estimated by this department. Out of 53,934 dead letters held for postage, mis-directed, &c., which, though not containing valuable enclosures, were sent out for delivery, but 4,466, less than one-twelfth, were not delivered, because refused, or for other causes, and were again returned to the dead letter office. It is true that with dead letters of all kinds the proportion returned a second time to the department would be somewhat larger; but if it were increased to one-fourth of all dead letters sent out, the return to the writers of all such correspondence, susceptible of restoration, would involve no additional expense to the department, while it would be generally gratifying and often extremely useful to the public. About 2,500,000 dead letters are annually received, and, excluding letters without the signature or address of the writers, and those containing circulars and manifestly worthless matter, it is estimated that 1,500,000 could be returned to the post office of the writer. If one-fourth of these were refused or uncalled for, the department, under existing law, would receive from postages on the remaining 1,125,000 the sum of $33,750.

The number of clerks required to examine and send out 1,500,000 letters would not exceed twenty-five, and their compensation, at $800 per annum, which is deemed sufficient for the nature of the service to be performed, would amount to $20,000, leaving a net revenue to the department of $13,750.

In view of the encouraging results already attained, by the partial use of the unclaimed dead letter money for this purpose, I would respectfully recommend that authority be granted by Congress to employ the proposed clerks, and that $20,000 be appropriated therefor, in addition to the ordinary appropriation for officers and clerks in this department.

I would also suggest that valuable dead letters, when returned to their owners should be charged with treble the ordinary rate of postage, comprising one rate for return transportation to the dead letter office, one rate for registration there, and one rate for return transportation to the writers or owners. It has already been shown that the failure of such letters to reach their destination is rarely attributable to the department, while in their restoration much time and labor are expended, for which the ordinary letter postage is scarcely a sufficient recompense.

For the same reasons unregistered letters thus returned might be charged with double rates.

PRE-PAYMENT OF POSTAGE.

My predecessor called attention to the fact that large numbers of unpaid letters continued to be posted, notwithstanding the act of March 3, 1855, making pre-payment compulsory, and stated that the practice of notifying the parties addressed that such letters would be forwarded on receipt of postage, had been abandoned, because it appeared, after trial of more than five years, that the evil continued unabated, showing a determination on the part of many correspondents using the mails to evade the postal laws. By immediately sending this class of letters to the dead letter office, it was expected that a proper compliance with the law would be enforced, but so far from this being the case, the number after one year's trial exceeds ten thousand each month, and the attention they require imposes considerable additional labor and expense on this department.

The practical result of this decision of my predecessor is so different from what was anticipated, that I have been induced to revive the former regulation, requiring postmasters to notify persons to whom unpaid letters are directed, that they will be forwarded on receipt of the postage enclosed in a *paid* letter to the postmaster. Thus the number returned to the dead letter office will be reduced at least two-thirds.

The detailed statement of the expenditures, under the head of miscellaneous payments, required by the act approved June 15, 1860, will be found appended to this report, as furnished by the Auditor's office.

MISCELLANEOUS.

APPROPRIATIONS FOR CALIFORNIA OVERLAND MAIL.

I have in a previous part of this report alluded to the refusal at the treasury to pay the appropriation for the overland mail service to California. It seems to me so evidently to have been the purpose of Congress to require the payment of the amount stipulated from the treasury, under the 9th and 11th sections of the act, that I again call the attention of Congress to the subject for such further legislation as may be required. It certainly cannot be supposed that a con tract of that magnitude could be required by postal interests alone. The general interests of the country required it, and the compensation should therefore be made by a general appropriation from the treasury, as this department presumes to have been the intention of the law.

THE POST OFFICE BUILDING AT NEW YORK.

Owing to the extraordinary demands upon the treasury for the maintenance of the higher interests of the country, I have not deemed it prudent to proceed, at present, with the erection of a new building for the New York post office.

The balance of the appropriation heretofore made for that purpose, after paying for the site purchased, remains therefore unexpended.

THE POST OFFICE BUILDING AT PHILADELPHIA.

In view of the pressing need of improvements in the post office accommodations at Philadelphia, and in connexion with the structure designed for both post office and United States court rooms, the commission invited plans and proposals for adapting to these uses the building which has been already purchased. This has resulted in the offer of a plan which appears to me satisfactory; and which, in my judgment, will answer the purposes proposed for many years to come, and will also meet the demands of good taste and convenience, at a cost not exceeding $30,000, for which the existing appropriation is sufficient. The question of its acceptance is now pending before my associates, as provided by law of the last Congress.

BOSTON POST OFFICE.

I have made arrangements by which the post office in the city of Boston has been restored to its former site, on State street, without additional expense to the department. It was done the more cheerfully because it enabled me to signify my reprobation of the conduct of a public officer using the influence of his official position to promote his private ends, in disregard of the public interest. This order, it is also believed, was in accordance with the wishes of a decided majority of the business interests affected by it. In connexion therewith I was able to terminate the claim on the fund of $12,600, formerly deposited by certain parties, for the return of which, after deduction of the expenses of one removal each way, Congress passed an act approved March 2, 1861. The sum of $9,584 84, was required to cover the double rent accrued during the period when the first removal was suspended. In my judgment this was to be deducted, as it was expressly understood it should be at the time of the contract of indemnity. The settlement was effected on this basis, and the sum of $3,015 16 was returned under that provision of law, and the account closed.

PROPOSED AMENDMENTS OF THE LAW.

By the act of Congress, approved July 2, 1836, (5 Stat., p. 84, sec. 33,) it is provided that the appointment of postmasters at offices where the commissions allowed to postmasters amounted to one thousand dollars or upwards in any one year, terminating on the 30th day of June, should be made by the President, with the advice and consent of the Senate.   In several cases offices which have once earned that amount in one year have subsequently fallen below it, and become permanently reduced in value.   Doubts have existed whether, by the letter of the law referred to, the appointment nevertheless did not continue to be presidential.   It is recommended that this doubt be removed by an amendment to the law providing that the appointment shall cease to be presidential whenever such commissions shall have been ascertained to be less than the sum of one thousand dollars for the fiscal year next preceding an appointment.

THE POSTMASTERS FRANKING PRIVILEGE.

The franking privilege is in this country greatly extended.   In the United Kingdom, the only other country in which very low rates of inland postage prevail, it appears to be limited to addresses and petitions to the Queen, and petitions to either house of Parliament.   All other mailable matter is chargeable with postage.   Hence, in part, the success there of the low postage system in point of revenue.

In this country, however, it is extended to cover a large class of postmasters, probably the majority.

By the first section of the act approved March 2, 1847, each deputy postmaster, whose compensation for the last preceding year did not exceed two hundred dollars, may send through the mails all letters written by himself, and receive all addressed to himself on his private business, free of postage, the weight not exceeding a half ounce.

This privilege is greatly abused, and ought to be revoked.   If other compensation is due to a postmaster beyond his commissions, it should be in the discretion of the Postmaster General, not exceeding ——— per cent. additional to that now allowed, that it may go to the intelligent and faithful, not to the shrewd and unscrupulous, as it chiefly does under the existing law.   Privileges resting in the conscience of the recipient, as to their extent, are dangerous.

I recommend the repeal of this clause, conferring the franking privilege on postmasters whose commissions do not exceed two hundred dollars ; only letters certified to be on post office business shall be allowed to be sent or received by postmasters, free of postage, and this enforced by proper penalties.

COLLECTION OF POSTAGE ON PRINTED MATTER.

Great losses to the postal revenue arise from the neglect of postmasters to collect the postage, as required by law, on printed matter, both transient and periodical, sent through the mails.   It is known to have been left in arrear for years.

The rates on transient printed matter, and on that sent to regular subscribers, are different, being higher on the former.

The evil, it is believed, will be greatly remedied by an enactment providing that each copy of printed matter upon which the postage for at least one quarter shall not have been prepaid, either at the office of mailing or of delivery, shall be rated as transient matter, and the postage thereon collected on the delivery of each copy.

Power should also be given to the department to fine, at the discretion of the Postmaster General, not exceeding the sum of five dollars for each offence, any postmaster who shall deliver, without payment of postage as required by law, any printed matter arriving through the mails at the office of delivery, and to charge the same in his account, to be deducted from his commissions. It is believed that by these two provisions a large amount of revenue, now lost, will be saved to the department.

NAVAL LETTERS.

It is suggested for the consideration of Congress whether the privilege, by the act of the late session, conferred upon soldiers, to send letters without prepayment of postage, should not be extended to sailors and marines in the actual service of the United States, under such regulations as the department shall provide.

MAIL-CARRIER'S FEE.

By the act approved March 3, 1825, (section 20,) it is provided that a mail-carrier shall receive and deliver for mailing at the next office any letter delivered to him for that purpose more than a mile from such office. He is entitled for such carriage to demand and receive one cent from the postmaster for this service. Under the prepayment system now adopted, this provision should be amended so as to allow him to demand this fee of the writer, in money, and of the postmaster only when the letter shall bear a prepaid stamp for one cent additional to the postage.

NEWSPAPERS.

By the existing law, (section 16 of act approved March 3, 1845,) "newspapers" are declared to embrace printed matter issued by numbers, and published monthly, and are entitled to the same privilege of free exchanges and low rates of postage as daily and weekly newspapers enjoy. It is ascertained that this classification is abused by the publication of monthly issues of printed matter chiefly designed as an advertising circular, or to procure free exchanges for the proprietor, and they are often sent gratuitously.

I recommend that the definition of a newspaper, as given by that act, be amended by substituting the words, *published at short stated intervals of not more than one week*, for the words, "published at short stated intervals of not more than one month." Also, that the privilege of free exchange of publications be limited to newspapers as thus defined, and literary, educational, or religious periodicals, published not less frequently than once a month.

It is found that considerable frauds are perpetrated upon the revenues of the department by publishers of newspapers, who include, mingled with the packages sent to their regular subscribers, numbers of their issues which are not sent to their regular subscribers, and which are, therefore, subject to postage as transient matter.

To remedy this evil, I recommend that discretion be given to the head of this department to exclude, temporarily, from the mails any newspaper or periodical whose proprietors or agents shall send any of their issues without prepayment of postage to other than *bona fide* subscribers; or, otherwise, that an express penalty be imposed for such act.

CONGRESSIONAL POST ROUTES.

It is frequently found expedient, in connexion with the progress of railroad communications or changes of principal transportation routes, to change the termini of congressional mail-routes intersecting them.

I suggest, for the consideration of Congress, the propriety of expressly authorizing this department to change the termini and lines of congressional mail-routes, intersecting principal routes on which the mails are carried daily, whenever the postal service can be thereby improved.

ADDITIONAL MAILABLE MATTER.

The 12th section of the act of 1861 declares sundry additions to matter which may be sent through the mails. Various applications have been made to include other like matter, not expressly named therein, as mailable matter.

It is suggested whether it would not be expedient to invest the department with the discretion to allow such other matter to be transmitted through the mails, at corresponding rates of postage, as the Postmaster General shall by order designate and allow. The public convenience and the revenues of the department would derive benefit from such discretionary power.

CARRIER'S FEE.

I renew the recommendation of my predecessor, that power be given to the department to regulate the carrier's fee, not exceeding the amount of two cents for the delivery of each letter. It cannot be sustained in some of the cities and districts without an increased rate. So long as it is discretionary with the party addressed to employ the services of the carrier or not, no just reason is perceived why the former discretion should not be given for the purpose of facilitating so important a branch of the postal service.

BRANCH OFFICES.

Requests have been made from several cities for the establishment of branch offices for the receipt and delivery of letters auxiliary to the city post office. I have been unwilling to establish them without some provision being made to meet the additional expense, for which the same fee allowed to carriers, one cent, would be sufficient. By the law authorizing their establishment (1847, chapter 63, §10) no charge is permitted for this additional service. I respectfully suggest, for the consideration of Congress, the propriety of amending that law and of granting this authority; and also of investing this department with the authority to erect in any city box-pillars for the receipt of letters to be mailed, to be thence collected by carriers, for which the fee of one cent each letter shall be prepaid by stamps.

CODIFICATION OF POSTAL LAWS.

A revised code of the postal laws, bringing together in proper arrangement the various statutes now gathered only by the examination of the legislation of many years, would greatly facilitate the performance of their duties by the numerous officers and agents attached to this department. This subject is respectfully commended to the attention of Congress.

RAILROAD SERVICE.

In the last annual report of my predecessor mention is made of the refusal or neglect of a large number of railroad companies engaged in the conveyance of mails to execute the contracts required by law of all contractors for the performance of their duties. This abuse continues. When a railroad is constructed through a district of country, competition in the conveyance of passengers, mails and merchandise, ceases on the route. Demand is immediately made for the mails, and without reference to the importance of the offices to be supplied, at a compensation much above that previously paid for coach and horse service. Increased speed is the only advantage which the service gains, although with respect to private business this is invariably accompanied with a great reduction of cost. The subject demands attention from Congress, and that measures be adopted to enable the government to contract on fair terms with these companies. The existing rates of compensation are in my judgment too high, and even at such rates the government is at the mercy of the companies. The government has the power to compel them to carry the mails at fair rates, as it has the right to the use of all private property necessary for its purposes, upon making just compensation; and provision should be made to resort to this power when fair arrangements cannot be made by way of contract. This would enable the department to deal with the companies on equal terms.

8 M

CHANGE OF CONTRACTS FOR DISLOYALTY.

Soon after the commencement of my term of office the country felt the shock of internecine arms. In view of the great crime attempted against the existence of the nation, it became the duty of this, in common with the other departments of the government, to put forth all its energies to prevent the consummation of that crime. By the existing laws all postmasters and mail-carriers, and all other persons engaged in handling the mails of the United States, or in clerical service, were required to take the usual oath of allegiance to this government, as well as for the faithful performance of their duties. Whenever it was made apparent by their declarations, or by their conduct, that there was a practical repudiation of the obligation of this oath, whether the party was a postmaster or a postal contractor, I ordered a removal from office in the one case and the deprivation of contract in the other. Not only was it unsafe to intrust the transportation of the mails to a person who refused or failed to recognize the sanctions of an oath, but to continue payment of public money to the enemies of the government and their allies, was to give direct aid and comfort to treason in arms. I could not thus permit this branch of government to contribute to its own over-throw. No other course could have reasonably been expected by such contractors. The *bona fide* observance of that oath, and the duty of allegiance itself, entered into and became a condition, a part of the consideration, of the contract itself. This failing, the department was equitably and legally discharged from its literal obligations. Protection on the part of government, and allegiance on the part of the citizen, are correlative, and are conditions mutually dependent in every contract, and the highest public interest demanded the rigid enforcement of this rule of action. Occasional local and transient inconvenience resulted of necessity, but far less than would reasonably have been expected. Loyal men, everywhere, sustained this action, and speedily furnished the requisite means for continuing the service without increased expense. These changes were mainly called for in parts of Virginia and Maryland, and in Kentucky and Missouri.

In the same, and in neighboring districts, the duties of the appointment office have been very onerous, from the great number of changes required in post offices, according to changing phases of public sentiment, individual action, and military occupancy. It is believed that these positions, with rare exceptions, are now held by men of unquestioned loyalty. Where such men could not be found, the offices have been discontinued rather than they should be held by repudiators of public faith, and used for purposes hostile to the perpetuity of our national institutions.

DISLOYAL PUBLICATIONS EXCLUDED FROM THE MAILS.

This department was also called upon to act upon another question, alike novel and important. Various newspapers, having more or less influence within the sphere of their circulation, were represented to be, and were in fact, devoting their columns to the furtherance of the schemes of our national enemies. These efforts were persistently directed to the advancement of hostile interests, to thwart the efforts made to preserve the integrity of the Union, and to accomplish the results of open treason without incurring its judicial penalties. To await the results of slow judicial prosecution was to allow crime to be consummated, with the expectation of subsequent punishment, instead of preventing its accomplishment by prompt and direct interference.

The freedom of the press is secured by a high constitutional sanction. But it is freedom and not license that is guaranteed. It is to be used only for lawful purposes. It cannot aim blows at the existence of the government, the Constitution, and the Union, and at the same time claim its protection. As well could the assassin strike his blow at human life, at the same time claiming that his victim should not commit a breach of the peace by a counter blow. While, therefore, this department neither enjoyed nor claimed the power to suppress such treasonable publications, but left them free to publish what they pleased, it could not be called upon to give them circulation. It could not and would not interfere with the freedom secured by law, but it could and did obstruct the dissemination of that license which was without the pale of the Constitution and law. The mails established by the United States government could not, upon any known principle of law or public right, be used for its destruction. As well could the common carrier be legally required to transport a machine designed for the destruction of the vehicle conveying it, or an inkeeper be compelled to entertain a traveller whom he knew to be intending to commit a robbery in his house.

I find these views supported by the high authority of the late Justice Story, of the Supreme Court of the United States. He says, in commenting on that clause of the Constitution securing the freedom of the press :

"That this amendment was intended to secure to every citizen an absolute right to speak or write or print whatsoever he might please, without any responsibility, public or private therefor, is a supposition too wild to be indulged in by any rational man. This would be to allow to every citizen the right to destroy at his pleasure the reputation, the peace, the property, and even the personal safety, of every other citizen. A man might, out of mere malice or revenge, accuse another of the most infamous crimes; might excite against him the indignation of all his fellow citizens by the most atrocious calumnies; might disturb, nay, overturn all his domestic peace, and embitter his parental affections; might inflict the most distressing punishments upon the weak, the timid, and the innocent; might prejudice all a man's civil and political and private rights; and might stir up sedition, rebellion, and treason, even against the government itself, in the wantonness of his passions, or the corruption of his heart. Civil society could not go on under such circumstances. Men would then be obliged to resort to private vengeance to make up the deficiency of the law; and assassinations and savage cruelties would be perpetrated with all the frequency belonging to barbarous and cruel communities. It is plain, then, that the language of this amendment imports no more than that every man has a right to speak, write, and print his opinions upon any subject whatever, without any prior restraint, so always that he does not injure any other person in his rights, person, property, or reputation ; *and so always that he does not thereby disturb the public peace, or attempt to subvert the government.*"

Of the cases presented for my action, upon the principles above named, I have, by order, excluded from the mails twelve of these treasonable publications, of which several had been previously presented by the grand jury as incendiary and hostile to constitutional authority.

I have the honor to be, &c., &c., your obedient servant,

M. BLAIR, *Postmaster General.*

To the PRESIDENT *of the United States.*